The Beginner's Guide to

DARKNESS

This Book will Help you to Find the Light

GEOFF THOMPSON

THE BEGINNER'S GUIDE TO DARKNESS

Published by:
Geoff Thompson Ltd
PO Box 307
Coventry
UK
CV3 9YP

www.geoffthompson.com

Printed and bound in Great Britain

ISBN: 978-0-95692-150-5

*Dedicated to my beautiful wife Sharon, with
love and light and toasted tea cakes.*

*Thank you to lovely Margaret Ring for the title of this book.
Big love and thanks to my gorgeous son
Louis for supplying my inspiration.*

Also by Geoff Thompson:

Red Mist
Watch My Back: The Geoff Thompson Autobiography
The Elephant and the Twig: The Art of Positive Thinking
The Great Escape: The 10 Secrets to Loving Your Life and Living Your Dreams
Fear – The Friend of Exceptional People: Techniques in Controlling Fear
Shape Shifter: Transform Your Life in 1 Day
The Formula: The Secret to a Better Life
Stress Buster: How to Stop Stress from Killing You
Dead or Alive: The Choice is Yours
Everything That Happens To Me Is Good
Everything that Happens To Me Is Great

'Now is the time for you to rouse yourself',
The master said; 'for sitting on a cushion
Is not the way to fame, nor staying in bed'.

Dante, *The Divine Comedy*

Contents

Prologue

I have just come off the phone. I was talking with a close friend who is presently unhappy because life has offered him an opportunity to grow, a chance to experience more freedom in his life, but he has chosen to see this opportunity as a hindrance, a blight on his day, his week – actually, he has chosen to see this exciting prospect as a black mark on his entire existence. My friend, who I love very much, is similar to many people I encounter. He wants more from life, but he is not prepared to add the extra labour to get it. He wants for lottery without work, he seeks health without sacrifice and he begs growth without discomfort. And when his desired booty is not delivered, free of charge and tied with a pink ribbon, he shapes his index finger into a gun, gathers a (seemingly infinite) stockpile of blame-bullets and starts making targets out of anyone (and everyone) within shooting range.

But what he does not do is point the finger of blame at himself.

My friend is in a dark place. A place of unknowing and ignorance. And the more I look around me the more I see that there are a plethora of folk inhabiting similar dark realities, places that no longer hold an anabolic purpose, but neither do they offer an obvious exit. *The Beginner's Guide to Darkness* is designed to help people who are not only ready to see the way out, but who are also prepared to take it. Because knowing is never enough. In the world of personal transformation, doing is all.

This book is for those who are tired of working out, and are brave enough to start working in.

Once you start working in you can make your wildest dreams a living reality, and even your darkest realities can become a catalyst for light.

Introduction

So what is darkness? And why do we need to understand it and escape its insidious grasp?

Darkness is any situation that makes you feel trapped. It's every difficult place in your life that does not appear to offer a positive outcome.

When I was locked into a glut of menial jobs and desperately wanted to become a writer, but was told cruelly to be realistic and stop dreaming – that was darkness.

When my first marriage lost its love, separation was a scary thought and divorce was both a distant dream and a (seemingly) immediate impossibility. I felt there was no escape, and leaving the spent relationship, whilst greatly desired by me, was a mountain too high to contemplate, let alone ascend.

This was darkness in the extreme. For me, for my ex-wife and for my in-the-middle-of-it-all children.

And when I found myself working and living in a seductively violent world that I desperately wanted to exit but felt helplessly unable to leave, it was a very dark place indeed.

There are many kinds of darkness, metaphoric prisons that do not need tangible bars to keep you locked in, invisible gaols that keep us from experiencing life to the fullest. Addiction (in all its forms), envy, jealousy, grudge, greed, illness and ignorance all hold people in dark and cavernous realities.

What I have learned from my earthly sojourn thus far is this: every dark place hides a secret doorway to a light reality.

Information and right action are all that are needed to escape.

That is why I wrote this book. To pass on the hard-won knowledge that has enabled me to die to the old and hackneyed and be born again to the new and infinite.

But be warned. This information will give you the key to open new doors, but knowledge brings its own pressure that demands we utilise the new-found data. A powerful impulse is born with new knowledge and that impulse is towards change. Ignorance is often seen as bliss, and many of us hide behind it because it is easier than looking at truth, which by its very nature demands that we challenge the status quo. Once you know the truth, there can be no hiding from it. Also, of course, knowing is never enough. Knowing is only the first stage. Many people understand these matters theoretically. And more still teach their theories to other seekers. But knowing without doing is impudent. Teaching others what we have not yet accomplished ourselves is like an ant pretending to lead an elephant. You have to use what you know. To use what you know takes courage. And courage is a skill best developed through practice, not theory.

On my travels through life (having been around a few corners, as the Irish say), I've seen many folk living in a dark existence, inhabiting the wrong body, living with the wrong partner, driving the wrong car and living the wrong life. They falsely convince themselves that this is as good as it gets!

This book is the first step towards shattering this disempowering premise, and proving that life can be infinitely better. It offers pragmatic advice on creating light by understanding dark. It is written by a man (me) who has experienced more adversity in one lifetime than most would see in ten, but who has learned (through hard labour and deliberate suffering) how to find light in even the darkest of places.

This is an exciting time to be alive. There are so many amazing opportunities, there is so much potential. I pray that this book helps you to realise this and to leave your dark abode and head – if not immediately into the light – then at least towards it.

Chapter 1

Lost and Found

There is a truth that I discovered very early on in life. I found it at a time when fear was disabling me and crushing my dreams. It wasn't just because the fear was so caustic, but rather it was because I was not acknowledging the fear. I was a man immersed in darkness who pretended to be bathing in light. When I was faced with things that scared me, rather than admit that I was scared I would lie to myself (and others) and say things like: 'I'm not scared of it (whatever it might be), I just don't want to do it.' Like a smoker claiming that he could give up cigarettes 'any time I want to', then adding (the ultimate statement of denial): 'I just don't want to!' If you are to be found (metaphorically), you first have to acknowledge that you are lost. How can you be cured of an illness if you don't even accept that you are sick?

The very moment you admit that you are lost, the universe will conspire to help you find your way. A portal will open and light will shine through your darkness. My success in life did not really begin until I sat down one day after a particularly bad depression (triggered by my inability to negotiate or even acknowledge change) and admitted to myself that, actually, I was really scared. Not of one or two things, I was scared of everything. And I felt like such an utter and despicable coward! I was sure I was the only man in the entire universe who was ever this scared (I had a tendency at the time to exaggerate a little). The first time I admitted to myself that I was scared, I fully and entirely expected to feel disempowered, as though the admittance of fear was the admittance of impudence. I thought that acknowledging that I was fearful might leave me vulnerable to more pain, and open me up to an avalanche of terror. I thought this revelation would validate, once and for all, my status as the class coward. I was delighted to find that the opposite was true. The moment I acknowledged (what I felt was) my weakness, I was completely empowered. I suddenly realised that in accepting responsibility for the way I felt, I enabled myself. If the problem was with me then the solution was also with me. And that was the moment my life changed forever and for the better. Every fear that I could admit was a fear that I could take control of, face and overcome. So I started to look at every aspect of my life that scared me (which was – as I said – every aspect). On a sheet of paper I wrote down the fears I felt were disabling me, and systematically started to face them one by one, again and again, until they dissolved.

Every fear, every bad habit, every addiction, every limiting belief represented a dark place to me. I created light by facing the fear. I changed the bad habits by replacing them with good habits. I killed the addictions and obliterated my limiting beliefs by finding evidence to disprove them. For example, if I believed that it was not possible for ordinary people (like me) to become writers or professional martial artists then I would find evidence to the contrary. The world is filled with ordinary people who have done extraordinary things. Then, of course, with inspiration as my fuel, I would go out and actually do the things that I felt were not possible. I became a professional martial artist. I became a writer. Once I had achieved what I felt was impossible my belief system expanded and my horizons widened. Suddenly bigger things seemed possible, actually everything seemed possible. Even my wildest dreams seemed within easy grasp. And of course they were. There are no impossible things. Only things that seem impossible.

I did this firstly with information. I became a voracious reader. If there was a book about anyone who had experienced or achieved what I was aiming to achieve – especially if I thought, or had been told, that it was not possible – I read it. Then I went out and put the new-found information to work and – with practice – I became a voracious doer.

Darkness is a state of not knowing. Darkness is also a state of knowing but not doing.

Darkness is only transformed into light with action and courage. Darkness is uncertainty, but certainty does not exist without action. There is a time to stop talking and reading and philosophising and researching and start doing.

Now is that time.

Other people's success is a good place to start. It is inspiring, it is mind-expanding, but there will be a part of you that will always think: 'Yea, but that's them. They're gifted. They're lucky. They had a better start in life. They were in the right place at the right time.' A part of you will never really believe that the impossible is possible until you achieve it yourself. There is no real proof, other than your own success.

That is what I set out to do. Create my own light. Be my own proof. So the kid who dreamed of being a professional martial artist suddenly was one. I found myself running down the road at six in the morning (my morning training session) with this big smile on my face and thinking: 'This is my job. This is what I do for a living.' Of course I built on my success (because success leads to success leads to more success) until, ultimately, I reached the world stage and was voted the number one self-defence author in the world. And the young aspirant who dreamed of becoming a writer? All I needed to do was sell one piece of work and I could consider myself a professional scribe, and from that I could build an entire universe. My first article was sold to a martial-arts magazine. It might not seem like much looking from the outside in, but what it did for me was pivotal: it disproved the lie that 'people like us' cannot become professional writers. Once that lie had been shattered, the word 'limit' suddenly disappeared from my vocabulary. I followed up the article with a book (me! A published author). And one book led to thirty-five published books, thousands of articles, a staged, toured play and a £2,000,000 feature film about my life.

The lie is the darkness. Expose the lie. Look for evidence to the contrary. This will inspire you. Be the ultimate proof by achieving the impossible, then use the foundation of your new truth to build an empire.

This process is an epic journey. It is one that you and I intend to travel. It has to start somewhere, and that somewhere is here. That somewhere is now.

So if you feel lost, acknowledge that you are lost. A portal will open; you will see light, usually in the form of new information. Absorb the information.

But as I said, seeing light is not the same as stepping out of the dark. It is not information that frees us, it is wisdom, and wisdom is information in action.

OK! So what then? You admit you are lost, a portal opens, you see some light but (and this happens a lot) for whatever reason you do not take advantage and exit and you think that you may have missed your chance. But you didn't miss your chance. What you did was, you learned how to create light. You learned how to create an opening from where you are through to where you would like to be.

So do it again.

And this time, step up, step out, and walk through the portal, out of that shit job, away from your caustic relationship, into that healthy body.

If you can open one portal of light, then you can open a second portal of light (actually, you can open as many as you like). If it opens a second time and you still don't take it you need to ask yourself a question.

Why didn't you take it?

There can be only one reason. Fear!

You can dress it up any way you like, but the bottom line is that it is still fear. From your old dark reality you reached the doorway, but that doorway was guarded, and the guard was fear, and the fear created feelings of discomfort. So you backed into the dark where you may have been lost, but at least you felt safe. I have done this so many times in this incarnation that I have lost count. I once spent seven years working shifts (early mornings, afternoons and nights) in a chemical factory and I have to tell you that I hated it. Twenty-five years later I still have nightmares about being back there. That was how bad it was. I was offered many good chances to leave that dark employ, each one more fulfilling, but every time I turned it down. Because of fear. At the time, I said it was because the money was not good enough, or the timing was wrong, or my wife preferred me on shifts (there is always a long list), but the bottom line was that I was scared. I retreated back into what I hated but what was familiar. I was too scared to leave. I was too scared of change.

The first two times that I was offered the chance to become a professional martial artist I baulked. I didn't flat out admit that at the time – I think I pretended that the timing was wrong (it always is, I find, especially when you're scared), or that I needed a bit more money, or a few more students – but the bottom line is I created two separate exit portals, and I did not take either of them. But, even though I had not yet taken the exit, I had found a way out. And on the third attempt I took the doorway from a dark factory job into the world of professional martial arts teaching. And I have to tell you that it was a delight. I was teaching martial arts as my job. How good is that! I was training eight hours a day and for years and years afterwards I would find myself thinking: 'I can't believe that this is my job.' And, of course, once I found a way out of the conventional working life, lots of my friends, having seen me do it, followed suit. Once I had overcome my fear, it helped them to overcome their fear. It made their exit easier because they had witnessed mine first-hand.

I have exited many dark realities and entered more new ones than I can count, and this is what I have learned about fear.

Fear is not a guard. Fear is a guide.

It is not trying to stop you from leaving; it is waiting to escort you through the doorway. You think fear is your nemesis. Fear is your friend.

So, if you missed the second and the third exit, try again. Be brave when the feelings of fear and discomfort come. Give yourself to them. Let them carry you into the new reality.

You may be asking at this point (I would be): 'Why should I trust you? Why should I believe what you are saying?'

You shouldn't. You shouldn't trust a word I am saying, or a word anyone says for that matter. But you should listen to my words. Then you should cross-reference my advice with your own experience, with your intuition. Or better still put the words into action. Be your own proof. And, if you want further validation, match my words with every bible and every philosophical tablet.

Fear is not the enemy. Fear is the friend. The words are true.

So, try again, and keep trying until you make it work. You only have to create light from a dark situation once, then you will know how to do it forever. Like riding a bike, once you learn you will never forget.

If you are still feeling unsure, look around you. I know it's dark, but you can see that you share your darkness with many others. Only the few find light. Actually that's not entirely true. Many find the light then switch it off again because of fear, because of the feelings, because fear is the enemy.

Winston Churchill said that many people stumble upon the truth, but they get up and walk away as though nothing happened. Perhaps this is because the truth is too simple, or too uncomfortable, or because truth is the harbinger of change, and we all secretly quake in the shadow of change.

You believe it must be true that fear is the enemy because everyone says so. But the everyone that you are listening to are still in the dark, still lost. So why ask the lost for directions? Why ask the blind to lead? If all the lost souls are saying that fear is the enemy, what does that tell you? Perhaps they are wrong?

When I was extremely unhappy, stuck in an oily, dirty, engineering factory (thinking: 'There must be more to life than this'), I asked my workmates if they knew the way out. They universally informed me that I should be grateful for my job sweeping floors. It was a cushy number, a job for life, a job (apparently) the likes of which did not grow on trees (thank fuck for that!). And for several years I believed them. Why would they lie? And for more years I remained safe (I thought) but unhappy. Then one day I looked around me, at the other guys working in the factory, the other folk sharing my dark reality, and I realised that my advisers all looked absolutely fucking miserable. And this made me question their sage advice. My questioning of their advice, of their truth, created a spark of light for me. If this job was so sterling why were they all so pig-miserable? So I asked one of the machinists how long he had been working in the factory. He told me that he had been there for thirty years. I asked him if he was happy. He looked at me as though I had just French-kissed his mother and said: 'No! I hate the fucking place.' And that is when I realised that you do not ask advice about diamonds from a lathe turner. That proved to be the catalyst I needed. I left the factory, never to return. Was I scared? Yes. Terrified. But I was also very excited. I had achieved what other folk had failed to do in thirty years, and not because I had overcome fear, rather because I had embraced fear. I found a way out, and the way out was good. Later, lots of my friends followed me through the same portal. And it was good for them too.

So, dear reader, do me a huge favour. Create some light. A spark. Open a portal by questioning what your reality is telling you. You've done it before. You know how to do it. Inspire open a portal of light. Now walk towards it and stop the moment you meet fear. Examine the feelings that come with fear. Sit in the feelings that come with fear. And know this: everything you want in the world, everything that you have ever desired, everything in existence that pleases you is residing just across the border, just past those feelings. Nirvana is just over the hill called fear. And know this too: those feelings (or rather being scared of those feelings) are the only single solitary thing that is keeping you in the dark. People think that finding light means a lot of learning, so much learning, too much learning, about too many things. Not so. You only have to learn one thing, courage. And, you only need to use courage in one area. Your feelings. When you stop fearing your feelings you will create perpetual light.

Chapter 2

The Feelings

About those feelings. When you walk toward the light, out of the dark, you meet fear. That is a given. It is a sign that you are on the right track because discomfort is always the prerequisite to growth. So you meet with fear and you feel uncomfortable feelings. And you automatically associate everything outside your dark world, your current reality (job, relationship, city, country, life), your comfort zone, with those feelings. But I have stepped through many portals and felt those feelings on many occasions and I can tell you categorically – one hundred per cent – that those feelings only exist on the very periphery of each reality. There is just a thin membrane of fear, a womb of discomfort. Once you break through it the feelings of discomfort dissipate, and are replaced by feelings of euphoria and joy and perpetual growth.

I will say that again because it is important. Darkness is a comfort zone that can be outgrown, and fear is a womb-boundary that is both necessary to birth a new reality, and is ephemeral. It does not last. Once you step through the portal, it is gone.

When I decided to give up my job and write full-time I was filled with the fear of failure, of success (could I handle it?), of poverty, and the fear of many more unnameable things. I created an opportunity to make my dream a reality, but once faced with the possibility of it becoming real I felt a sudden and overwhelming fear. And I imagined that everything outside of my current reality would be fearful and that, whilst I hated the job I was doing, at least it was safe, at least it was comfortable. But as soon as I took the next step and became a writer, all the feelings of fear disappeared, and suddenly I was in a new reality. Within a matter of weeks it was as though I had never done anything else, as though writing had been my job forever.

Fear does not last.

The same as everything else in this temporary universe, it has its time and then it is gone. And its time (I have found) is determined by you. The moment you fully commit yourself to a new reality and embrace the associated fear, it begins to dissipate.

Back to fear, the friend. It is a guide, not an enemy. It holds a message, not a curse. It is there to grow you, not destroy you. It is there to guide you through to the light, not scare you back into the dark. And it has a limited shelf-life that is determined by you.

Anticipation of confrontation is more painful than the confrontation itself.

People stay in anticipation longer that they need to because they fear to do the thing that they fear. Dare yourself. Confront it. Know that confronting and overcoming fear builds warriors.

In the darkness, hiding from the light, you find only worms. Pushing out of the darkness into the light, you find titans. Fear faced builds warriors. So face the fear. Know that there is no growth in comfort. Marinate in your feelings of fear because every second will temper you. It will build the armour you need to live the life that you intend.

Chapter 3

A Warrior's Armour

To leave the dark and brave the light you need new armour, a fresh skin. The old one has to be shed so we can grow. It is when we go through uncomfortable situations, when we go through fear, that our old skin is scorched off and shed. When we shed skins we feel vulnerable, scared and uncomfortable. But it is the vulnerability, the fear and the discomfort, that creates the need for, and indeed the growth of, our next skin. Our new skin is bespoke armour designed specifically and innately for whatever new reality we enter.

Let me give you an example. As a younger man I had a disabling fear of violent confrontation. To overcome it I took a job as a nightclub bouncer. The job was in a place called Coventry, which had been polled as the most violent city in Europe for its size and population. To survive in such a violent world I needed to shed my old skin (that had been designed specifically for the safe world of the factory worker), and create a new one. The gross fear associated with this kind of employ (on the nightclub doors) is very sharp and it does two wonderful things: it strips away the old skin, and – over a period of time – prepares you a new one. Within a relatively short period of starting on the doors as a bouncer, I developed a hardy armour that enabled me to work in an environment that asked everything, and often (for those who did not adapt) took everything. It was stepping through the membrane of fear that transformed Geoff the Factory Worker into Geoff the Bouncer. Stepping through shed the old skin and tailored the new. Similarly when I decided to become a writer I had to develop yet another skin, a different kind of armour. It was not one as war-like as the one needed in the world of physical violence, rather it was a skin (equally thick) that would protect and prepare me for the harsh rigour of a writer's employ. Writing is a fiercely competitive world and not one for the faint of heart. To succeed at the middle or top end (or at any end for that matter) of the writing business, you have to develop foot-thick skin and titanium nerves. The odds of becoming a published writer are so slight that, apparently, they do not even attract official odds. And I have never worked in a field that offered so much ambiguity ('We love your work, but we do not want to buy it') and so much uncertainty ('We think you are going to be huge, but we are not sure when'). The only way to cope is to develop, in your armoury, a high tolerance for both ambiguity and uncertainty, and a skin as thick as a whale sandwich so that the (often) relentless barrage of critical slings and arrows do not penetrate and damage your creativity.

When Carlos Castaneda was training under the spiritual mystic Don Juan Matus, the latter told him: 'Your reality is one room in a house of one hundred rooms. If you train with me I will show you how to access the other ninety-nine. In fact if you train with me I will show you how to get out of the house.'

Every new reality that you enter (and there are more than one hundred, in fact, there are as many realities as you can imagine) demands that you replace your old skin with a new one. The process of going from one room to the next is the process of shedding the old and growing the new. It is the fear that acts as the agent for both the casting off and the taking on. In other words it is a necessary pain. Exiting the dark for new light, going through that new birth, is a tempering process. It's uncomfortable, but it's good. Knowing it is good enables us to better cope with it. After all it is easier to take foul-tasting medicine if we know that it is going to do us good. We need to become so comfortable with this anabolic discomfort that eventually it is no longer uncomfortable.

Then rest!

All work and no fun makes for a very dull Johnny!

Chapter 4

Rest and Recuperation

All growth takes place during periods of rest. Work hard, push through pain, face your fear, stretch and strain, step into new realities – then rest. You must rest. If you don't rest, you may break. Certainly you will not grow.

Getting out of the dark of your reality (whatever that might be) is important, actually I would say it is vital, but it takes a lot of effort. Sustained effort uses a lot of energy and that energy needs to be renewed constantly. If it is not renewed, then like a car without oil and petrol, it will eventually break down.

On many a quest to find success in different areas I have failed to heed this lesson and have broken as a direct result. When I was fearful of violence and violent encounters I decided to break my fear by becoming a black belt in karate.

Currently I hold a multitude of black belts in different martial arts, but my initial fear came at a time when I was training for my very first black belt, in a Japanese system of karate called Shotokan. During my neophyte preparations I did not observe any limitations, and gave myself no boundaries. I got the work ethic right: I trained harder than anyone else, pushed harder than anyone else and I was relentless in my preparation. I intended to be so good at my grading that I could not fail. I was working long hours in the factory, often through the night, and yet I still trained two, often three times a day. I even trained at 2 a.m. (in my dinner hour on the night shift), as well as running to work, running home, even training during my work hours whenever I got a spare minute. The result was that I passed my grading with flying colours, then afterwards fell into a deep and prolonged depression. In retrospect I realised a great lesson. If you work hard, you need to rest and play hard too. I did the first, but badly neglected the second and third. I just trained. And trained. In my quest to win a new reality (the elusive black belt) I failed to heed the rules and rest. It was the equivalent of investing everything I had into climbing an Everest, but failing to leave myself the energy to make the heady climb back down. Do you know that you cannot claim to have ascended Everest unless you get up and down alive? More people have died on the descent of Everest than at any other point of the climb.

I learned that work without rest and play is false economy. I learned to discipline myself to stop and rest, knowing that it was the rest away from the fight that enabled me to re-fuel, take stock and sharpen my intent.

Some things take time. So give yourself time. And they always take a lot of effort. So respect the fact that effort is energy and energy needs a daily top-up. That top-up comes from rest and play. I used immense energy to reach my goal and win my first black belt, but I failed to top-up. As a consequence I burned out. It took me months to recover. I know other people who did not recover. I know many who were in too much of a hurry, did not respect the process and are no longer here to tell the tale. Often in our obsessive drive to create new realties we forget that this is a serious business, that our bodies and our minds are sensitive and need careful handling. I have been corresponding recently with a lovely lady who suffered badly with bullying and depression in her youth. This was her reality and it was dark. She felt that she would never be able to break free from this limiting life, but through knowledge and courage she did. And since then this lovely lady has overcome many fears and created a strong reality for herself in the fire brigade, something that she once felt she would never have the courage to do. But, due to the nature of her employ, she was exposed to many harrowing situations that triggered massive fear, each of which had a negative effect on her mentally. If she had been able to find respite in between each situation she would have, no doubt, been able to use these situations as a developing tool towards hardiness. But she wasn't. Like me she struggled on without rest until she was burnt out. Last time I spoke with her she was in a bad way. Her nerves were shattered and, unfortunately, she was in that dark place of looking for someone to blame.

There is no need to end up in this situation if you heed the process. Move forward. Take lots of breaks. Remember that you grow when you take breaks. Remember that you break if you do not.

So by all means be a demon for action, but make sure that you match your action with recuperation, or suffer the consequences.

And recuperation is also a great time and place for contemplation.

It was during a recent period of contemplation, when I sat in the dark and the quiet for a long period of time in order to rest my body and mind, that I discovered something amazing. I would like to share it with you. Often in the midst of the battle we get so caught up in the fight that we miss vital lessons. Only by stopping and taking time out do those lessons present themselves to you. This particular lesson, this very vital lesson, I call 'the secret'! Because of all the things I have learned thus far, this is the most exciting and the most intriguing.

Chapter 5

The Secret

During a particularly prolonged period of contemplation between battles, I discovered an amazing secret. It is one that has been validated by everyone from Rumi to the Buddha.

The secret will change your life forever.

The secret is this: the light you seek is within the dark you would escape. In fact, the light you seek is created by the dark you would escape. When I was terrified of life I ran from it, I hid from it, I covered in it blankets of medication and sense gratification (drink, alcohol, food, sex). When I got tired of running and hiding and escaping I tried another tactic. Instead of feeling fear and running in the opposite direction, I turned to face fear and welcomed it in. I realised that looking outside of myself for escape was futile. There is no help for you outside; there are only supporters, people cheering you on, people inspiring you. No one can pull you out, ease you out or coerce you out. You want people to pull you out, and you often want to pull people out when they are stuck, but it doesn't work like that. Even if you die for someone ten times you will not change their karma one bit. And if they die for you a hundred times, it will not change your karma one bit either. If someone pulls you out of the dark, you will end up right back in it again. You only really learn when you pull yourself out. And the same goes for other people. You cannot save them. You can enable them, guide them and inspire them, but you cannot save them. They have to save themselves. This is why you see so many people being pulled out of a bad situation by friends only to find that weeks (sometimes hours) later that person is right back in trouble again. Everyone is where they are meant to be. Everyone. Even if we do not want that to be true, it is. The moment it is not meant for them they will change it. Them, not you. This means that you are in the right place too. Even if you do not want to acknowledge it. And when you have harvested all you can from where you are, you will change where you are. And if you are at that point now (I presume you are – you are reading this book after all) this book will offer the perfect words at the perfect time. If you are not ready for change, then this book will most likely end up in the dustbin.

To reiterate: only you can create your own light.

If you keep lifting another man's bar-bell, he will never develop his own physique.

If you let other people continually lift your bar-bell, you will never grow your own physique.

So the main ingredient in creating light is darkness.

Read inspiring books, watch inspiring films, have motivational conversations that fire you up, but do not wait for any of these catalysts to free you. Only you can free you. We all already know everything we need to know about light: where it is, how to make it, how to stay in it. We just forgot. This is your (my) reminder.

As a young, naïve man I thought that darkness equalled evil.

Lesson one in all things dark: there is no evil. There is also no good or bad, just opposite energies. When you make yourself the resisting element between these opposing energies, light is created.

To place yourself between the two energies (like standing on the periphery of one reality, waiting to enter a new world) takes courage, because of those feelings again, those feelings that you don't like. If you can get used to those feelings you can create a lot of light. If you can become comfortable with those feelings you could create abundance.

If (and only the rare few manage to do this) you can learn to love those feelings, enjoy them, you will become the light master.

Light masters are beacons. People traverse the globe to touch the light master.

The dark is often associated with fear. We fear to leave old realities as much as we fear to enter new ones. I have a friend called Glenn who is a master boxing coach with his own successful gym, called The Red Corner. He is often seen as a fearless type. People view his success and say: 'Yea, but it's easy for you.' But it is not easy for Glenn, and it was never easy for Glenn. I can remember when he was working on the building site setting up scaffold. He spoke with me one day about his dream of escaping his cripplingly hard reality as a manual worker to instead spend his days teaching people the high art of pugilism. He had the skills – he had trained all his life – but he did not have the confidence. After all (he said), who was he to make his living teaching others? Many people (including me) offered him advice and inspiration. We showed him his potential and encouraged him towards it. We even showed him where the door was. What we could not do was walk through that door for him. Only he could do that. But he was afraid because leaving the building site was not simply a change of job. For him it represented a complete change of identity. And there was so much uncertainty involved that he was afraid to take the step. Eventually he dared himself and he did take the step. Suddenly this man of the ring had so many students that the room he hired to train them in was not big enough and he was forced to find his own premises to keep up with the demand (this happened over a period of years). So he found himself in the same position again. The reality that he now inhabited as a boxing trainer had become too small and he needed to access another identity, the identity of a gym owner. But who was Glenn Smith to think himself capable of running his own gym? What I asked him was this: who was Glenn Smith not to run his own gym? Presently Glenn runs an amazing gym that is fast becoming too small for his ambition, and before long

(I am sure) he will be looking for more light, for a new identity, and a better and better reality.

It was fear that kept Glenn on the building site. But ultimately, when he embraced that fear, it was fear that fuelled him and got him off it.

And let's make one thing clear about fear. People think that there are many different fears. In fact I have found that there is only one – fear of fear itself, fear of the fear feelings. But the way out is always through the feelings. So stop running away from the feelings. Instead of running away, creep, edge, shuffle, walk, jog or – if you are feeling particularly brave – run towards those feelings.

The masses cower in the face of fear. Many, many people place a blanket over their feelings with alcohol, drugs, food, gambling, pornography, people-pleasing, and materialism – but the feelings are still there, festering beneath the surface. The feelings want to talk to you. They want to share a secret.

The feelings can be your prison or they can be your escape.

The fear keeps us under lock and key – we think. Until we learn to stop running from the fear, the fear will always envelop us. We have to turn towards it. Within the fear we will find the doorway out.

Throw away the blankets. Your armour is your naked courage.

When you turn to face fear your three-dimensional monsters will become two-dimensional cartoons. And, under your glare, they will dissipate.

When you are in the dark, know that you are sitting on the raw material to make gold. And you are the alchemist!

The formula is simple. Information + courage x confrontation = light.

Don't be fooled. All fears are simply one fear with many cunning disguises.

Test it. This is what I did. Every time I found myself in a new situation that triggered fear I sat down, closed my eyes and located the very centre of the feeling, the very core. I stripped away the drama of the situation, the story, and concentrated purely on the feelings that it evoked. And at the very centre, the fear of becoming ill, the fear of failure, the fear of success, the fear of pain, the fear of loss and the fear of dying are all the same. The story might be different but the feelings that it evokes are exactly the same. The feelings, when we detach from the story, are little more than energy or fuel, and what you do with that fuel is entirely up to you. Imagine for one second that the fear-energy you experience is electricity (as a for instance). Electricity heats your house, it generates your light, it runs your computers, it cooks your dinners and, if you fail to show it respect it kills you dead. If you had a visitor from another planet who (for some obscure reason that I am making up for the sake of this example) received an electric shock, how difficult would it be to say to him: 'Actually, electricity is really very good. It can be put to a multitude of good, life-changing, even life-saving purposes. Honestly!' You'd have quite a job convincing him that electricity could be a force for good whilst he had 10,000 volts cooking his alien internal organs. From my vast exposure to fear and fearful situations, this is what I have learned about the energy of fear: if you respect it and use it and do not cower before it, this potent energy can fuel all your dreams. If you disrespect it, if you use it with folly, or worse still fail to use it at all, it will cook you alive. We all know that the feelings are uncomfortable, but as I said, this is a perception. If you embrace the feelings and kill the story, it is just fuel. What you do with that fuel is entirely up to you. And here is another concept, something that you might want to look at. It might help you to change your perspective on fear. Fear is arousal; it is the adrenals in action, releasing an emergency turbo blast of fuel to prepare the body for fight or flight. If you go into the centre of the feelings and kill the story, the fear is not fear at all, it is just feelings, fuel, literally adrenaline. Because we are not used to the feelings we panic when we experience them. We analyse the feelings and tell ourselves that we don't like them, that we don't want to feel them again. Our fear of the feelings does the opposite of what we want it to do. It triggers more fear (adrenaline). Suddenly we are awash in the stuff – and it is not healthy. What I have learned to do with adrenaline (fear) is to understand it and use it. I turn the feelings into action. I might make an article for a magazine with the feelings, they might fuel a five-mile run, or perhaps I will convert them into a day's work. If I am getting too much adrenaline, I will slow the flow down by deepening my breathing (this quietens the adrenals) and killing the story (this stops the adrenals – they love feeding on stories), or by fooling the brain into thinking that, actually, I am not afraid of the fear, in fact I want more. I find that when we consistently lie to ourselves about what we fear (in a positive way, that is, not in denial), if we keep telling ourselves that we like it (even though initially we don't), what we fear can become what we love. In this case, a lie told enough times can definitely become a truth.

Chapter 6

The Lie

What we fear most, we attract quickly. And there is no quicker way to attract fear and fearful situations than by running a continuous commentary in your head that says: 'I don't like this. I don't want this. I am scared of this.' So try reversing the internal commentary. Tell yourself: 'I do like this. I do want this. I want more of this, actually. I love this. Bring it on. More please.'

I learned this by accident. One day I was sitting in a vat of fear, anticipating all sorts of dire and disastrous things that might happen to me when (and if) an ex-partner left me. She was a nice girl and for a while there we had a grand life together. But life and time and contrasting ambitions caused a rift in our relationship that we both knew (at some level) was the harbinger of doom. I was rapidly expanding into new realities, and desperately trying to bring her with me, but her ambition did not extend beyond the boundaries of our back garden. As keenly as I was trying to grow, she was even keener to get me to either stay where I was or shrink. When I left the house to train (my dream was to become a professional martial artist at the time, but she wanted me to stay at the factory) she would threaten to change the locks if I left the house. She forced me to choose – her or the training. For a long time I was defeated by this bullying because I was afraid of being without her. Eventually though, the threats, the bullying and the imprisoning behaviour became tiresome. And it had the opposite effect on me. I was tired of being scared and fed up with being bullied. So one day, as I left the house to seek my ambition and she threw out the usual threat of: 'If you go now, I won't be here when you get back.' I said: 'You know what? I'm going. If you're not here when I get back that is up to you. Do your worst.' And I went. I didn't mean it of course. I didn't even believe it. But I said it convincingly enough for her to believe me (and after a few more occasions of saying it, I believed it myself). And I was scared. But when I got back she was still there and the locks were not changed. Her threats were empty. I got a cold back in bed for a week or so and the usual threat of 'your dinner is in the cat' for a week after that, but I had turned and faced my fear. I lied that I could handle whatever she threw at me ('Do your worst'), and eventually the lie became true.

Even if you don't believe it, say it anyway. Say it again and again and again until you do believe it. My friend Alan (a sterling man) was in the Foreign Legion where the conditions were relentless and the training savage (they were constantly preparing for warfare so you would expect no less). One of the hikes Alan did on a daily basis involved carrying a very heavy back-pack whilst running up hills. Everyone hated the hills. Without exception, it was the Legion anathema. The men talked about the hills, how they hated them, how they dreaded them, how they felt before, during and after, and how – after they left the Legion – they would be happy if they never hiked another hill for the rest of their lives. Alan knew that he had quite a long time left to serve in the Legion and decided that the best way to overcome the aversion to hill-hiking was to try and like it. So when everyone else was complaining that they hated the hills, Alan lied and said that he loved them. And when everyone did their utmost to avoid the hills, he did his utmost to court them at every opportunity. He was especially careful during the hill hikes themselves because that was the time – when the pain was hot and palpable – when his internal monologue automatically veered towards the negative. So when the pain was at its most intense and he wanted to scream ('I hate this!'), he overrode it and said to himself in a mantra: 'I love hills, I love hills, I love hills.' Now I cannot lie and tell you that the pain of climbing hills ever went away for Alan but I can tell you this – after a while he no longer had to lie to himself that he liked the hills, because suddenly he found that actually he did like them, in fact he loved them. And because he loved them he became good at them, the best, the top hill-hiker in the Legion.

My wife is a marathon runner. Part of her regular training is hills. She hated the hills. I told her about Alan and the Legion and his mantra of lies. So she tried it. She told herself that she loved the hills. She lied and said that the hills were exhilarating and that it was the best part of her training.

And now I cannot stop my wife from talking about how much she loves the exhilaration of hitting hills. She gets excited if we are out in the car and we see a hill, and if it is a particularly steep hill it is all I can do to stop her from getting out of the car there and then and running up it.

I was the same with re-writes when I first started screenwriting. You may or may not know that it is common in screenwriting to write many drafts of a piece before it is completed. I have often written dozens of drafts before finding a finished film. But I hated it, I hated it with a vengeance. And, of course, I thought a lot about the dreaded re-writes. I talked a lot about them and how much I hated them. Eventually re-writes became my anathema, to the point where I seriously considered sacking filmmaking for a writing employ that didn't involve so many re-writes. What changed my mind was when I started to look at other screenwriters, especially at the very successful and prolific ones. On observation I realised that all of them were brilliant at re-writes. They had mastered the art and in doing so had left all opposition trailing behind them. Re-writes were what separated the good from the great, and the great from the immortal. They had learned to love re-writes. So I modelled my behaviour on theirs. I started to lie to myself. I told myself how much I loved the re-writing process (it is actually amazing: some of the very best work comes during re-writes). I told others how much I loved it. In fact when I was working on a script and the producer or director said, 'You've done enough,' I found myself saying, 'Just one more draft, please.'

When you face fear, or pain, or whatever your anathema is, tell yourself that you love it, that you want more, that you can take ten times, twenty times more. Bring it on. It is anti-intuitive, but it works. And if it threatens you, like my ex threatened me, say: 'I don't believe you, you are a phantom.' Watch your fear fall. Watch its guard shatter. The guard we call fear will disappear and the guide will emerge and greet you like an old friend.

The concept is easy, we've established that, but I won't lie – darkness can be foreboding. Making light is no exercise for the sissy. It takes a warrior's courage and a steely spirit. So courage and spirit need to be developed. As I said (probably more than once), knowing is never enough, you need to *do*. It is the 'doing' that separates the wheat from the chaff.

Success demands that we enter through the narrow gate. Of the many called, only a few will enter.

Chapter 7

The Narrow Gate

In the Bible (Mathew 7:13–14), it says: 'Enter by the narrow gate; for wide is the gate and broad is the way that leads to destruction, and there are many who go in by it. Because narrow is the way which leads to life, and there are few who find it.'

Mathew is telling us that the gate (or portal) out of darkness is narrow, that many are called but few enter. And few enter because they are too fat to fit through the narrow gate. They are too (metaphorically) large because they are bloated with addictions. If we are to go through the way that leads to life, we need to go on an addiction-diet and shed the compulsions that keep us trapped in darkness. This is the foundation of self-control: control of the self. If you want to build a tower-block you need more than the base that your semi-detached is built on. If you want to build high then you need to dig your foundation deep and wide. The foundation is always the self, but the self is covered by so many layers of addiction that it is almost lost. The Kabala suggests that we are a species with immense and infinite power, but that our power is locked into our addictions. In order to get our power back we need to kill our addictions. Imagine that you are a billionaire, but all of your money is on loan to different people. Killing our addictions is the equivalent of calling in all of the debts.

To develop self, start with the self. All your power to create light is locked into the things you give yourself over to, the blankets we hide from the world under. So… your battle is with your addictions.

Many people (I was the same for a while) believe that they are not addicted, that they are in control of their vices. But you cannot flirt with your addictions. You either have them or you do not. And, whilst they are alive, they are a threat. Even subdued addictions are of the utmost danger. They wait patiently like vultures. They wait for a moment of weakness, the slightest gap, the smallest hole, to enter and take over. And with them, they bring the dark, the fear, the gaol that knows no depths.

Addictions hide light. Harbour them and eventually they kill light.

The number one addiction is comfort. It enters as a silk gown, envelops like a warm blanket and smothers like a straight jacket.

Comfort is the soul food of ego. And whilst ego reigns, the light cannot shine. Light will grow when ego is shrunk.

Light will reign when ego has gone. You shrink ego by taking away comfort, its soul food. Nothing will survive without sustenance. Withdraw the food, famish the ego.

My greatest fear as a younger man was the fear of success. I always feared my own potential. In my greatest moment I could see exactly where I could be and I felt awed by it, but at the same time my potential frightened me, often to the point where I withdrew and courted comfort instead. It was as though the unfulfilled desire for success was more reassuring than the success itself. I felt that where I was (the job, the relationship, the standard of health, the level of fitness) was not ideal, but it was known and it was safe. That somehow made it comfortable. I felt as though I could tread water and maintain the status quo. But you can't stay where you are, you cannot tread water, because there is no status quo. The universe is expanding all the time and to stay still is to shrink back, because everything else around you is growing. What I feared most about my potential was losing comfort. That's the bottom line. When I analysed it, that is what I was left with. I wanted more but I did not want to risk changing jobs, changing relationships, changing cars. For the very lazy even changing clothes everyday creates discomfort. When you take away comfort you feel deprived, as though taking on fresh challenges and seeking pastures new might mean that you will never be comfortable again. But this is the ego talking. When the addictions are killed and the ego is overcome you don't feel as though you are deprived. You feel as though you have escaped. Losing addictions is not about giving up your vices, it is about escaping them. When I was nearly sixteen stone and overweight I desperately wanted to lose three stone, but I didn't want to have to give things up (like cakes and beer) in order to do it. My ego presence felt deprived. Later when I had lost the addictions and with it the three stone in dead weight, I did not feel as though I'd given anything up. I felt as though I had escaped my insidious addictions. So from inside an addicted personality it does feel like you have to give things up (and this is why so many people fail to kill addiction because: 'Why should I give things up?'), but from the outside looking back in, having killed many addictions, it feels the opposite. It feels exhilarating. You look back and know that you have escaped.

And people presume that killing addictions will lead to a pleasureless existence. But that is a 'view from addiction', a comment from an addict looking from the inside out. Looking from the outside in you realise that you have not sacrificed addiction and comfort; you have escaped comfort and addiction. I was collared the other day by an old friend. Actually I say I was collared, I was pretty much assaulted. I was at the party of an old friend who was celebrating his birthday. Lots of my old friends were there. I had not seen them for many years and it was nice to catch up. But it was also sad to catch up, because many of my old mates had not moved forward in their lives at all. More than a few were harbouring some serious, life-threatening addictions. More worrying was the fact that they not only carried these addictions, but they defended their right to have them with all their might. Several years before, when I worked with these guys on the doors and in the factories, I felt and acted the same as they did. I had my addictions and I protected my right to have them with every sinew of my trapped body. But later, when I had learned a thing or two about darkness and how to escape it, I realised that I was trapped and fooled and I decided to do something about it. So I exited the dark reality that we all shared and went on to create a happy abundance for myself. My friends (most of them) stayed where they were. And that's OK, that is their journey. No judgment, no criticism. Everyone to their own. Anyway the night started well and I was really enjoying the company of some dear old mates. One friend in particular was very pleased to see me. We hugged, joked, talked about the past and shared a drink. He had a beer (or three) and I had a soft drink. I gave up alcohol many years ago as a part of my purification process and neither miss it nor think about it. I never announce it (people think that you are tilting a lance at them if you announce any kind of restraint or moderation); I never feel the need to. It is just what I do. I neither think about drink nor miss drink nor even notice that I am no longer drinking. But my friend noticed and took umbrage and before long (his addiction had taken hold by now and was doing the speaking for him) he began verbally (at one point viciously) attacking me because I did not drink and I did not smoke and I did not take drugs or watch pornography and I did not share my wife with other men (he liked to swing). He felt that because I had slaughtered my addictions my life was bland and I would go to my grave (well before him, he claimed at one point) unhappy and unfulfilled. He made the mistake that many people make. He believed that life without vice was a vicar's tea party, that it was bland and without colour or meaning. I told him that I killed my addictions because I needed energy, and I realised that all my energy was being spent on things that did not offer me any long-term profit. In fact they offered me a loss that was so great I could not even calculate it. I told him that I escaped my addictions in order to become free, to become an individual. Addictions (I told him) were for the sheep, and a follower I am not. At this point his aggression and his argument collapsed and he confessed that he really wanted to escape too, but he really liked his vices and he didn't want to give them up. I explained to my old friend that my life was immeasurably better without addiction – I have an amazing life. Dropping my sandbags of addiction has allowed me to fly high. I make my living doing only things that I love. I write books, for goodness sake, I make films, I can run for hours on end without getting out of breath, I traverse the globe, I sit in cafés till the early hours and talk philosophy with my heroes. I live the life of legend.

My point is this: you don't give anything up, you escape it. And you don't lose your fun, you find bigger and better fun.

There is no giving up. There is only escaping. But it is hard to see that through the miasma of addiction. You have to either trust the word of a former addict, or you have to take the information for a walk and be the proof yourself.

And you don't have to wait for tomorrow or the next day. You don't have to wait until next week or next year or the new year to start the journey. You can and you should start now. Because now is the only real time that you have control over.

In fact, why not do what I do? It is a technique for titans but it has always served me well. Don't wait for fear to knock on your door, go out and chase it down. Line your addictions up like ducks at a fair ground, and shoot them suckers down. This is what I like to call 'night travelling'!

Chapter 8

Night Travelling

The Sufi poet Rumi got it about right when he suggested that we go out into the night and hunt down our fears. The moon (he said) would shine for night travellers. The Bible says that if we walk towards God, God will run towards us.

In other words, God (the universe) helps those who help themselves. When you initiate growth it is as though the whole universe conspires to help you, and the most miraculous events will unfold, things you never thought possible, to help you escape the darkness of your current abode and create future abundance.

Write down all the things that create your dark, all your fears.

What is the one thing that scares you that is unique to them all?

Feelings.

Again we are back to feelings. Dark feelings. And what do those feelings threaten you with? More dark feelings. More of themselves. Control the feelings. Control yourself. Literally control the world.

If you control your thoughts about your feelings, you get to control the world because all things start with a thought. But when you try to practise your thoughts it often seems impossible, like trying to snatch at the wind. I used to read this ('control your thoughts') in books when I was facing difficult situations and think: 'Yea, that's all right, but how do you control thoughts? It's like trying to control time.' I realised later (after much practice and experimentation) that it is less about controlling your thoughts than it is about ignoring the thoughts that are not productive, nurturing the thoughts that are and deciding, as quickly as possible, which is which. I remember walking by the sea in Plymouth on one of my many visits there. I was on a prolonged book-signing tour and feeling exhausted. I was nervous about an upcoming talk I had to do in a bookshop. My fear-thoughts had found a life of their own and were multiplying at a grand rate. Every time I cornered one, another would pop up, and if I chased that, another thought came from behind, or from the side, or from underneath, until it felt as though I was colonised by thoughts that I neither wanted nor appreciated.

It was a particularly windy day; the gust was so strong that it was difficult to get out of its way. People were ducking into shops and doorways and cafés to escape the gale. The wind felt (I thought) very like my thoughts: powerful and beyond my control. I looked to see how the local seagulls coped with these very strong Atlantic winds, sure that they would have found a cove or a cave to hide in until the gale subsided. I was surprised to see that these Taoist masters of nature did not seek sanctuary at all. In fact they were hovering in the sky above me, right in the thick of the storm. It was an amazing sight to behold. They were not resisting the wind, nor escaping the wind, but actually sitting in the wind – riding it like sky-surfers. They were using the wind to assist effortless flight, stealing currents of air across the sky with grace and ease. So I tried the same with my thoughts. I didn't chase them. I didn't fight them. I didn't try to resist or direct or control them. I just observed them. I watched the flow of the 10,000 thoughts that came into my mind looking for a hook, but I gave them none. The part of me that was observing (I realised) knew that thoughts had no power unless they were engaged. I decided to practise not engaging with the thoughts. And when I did that, the thoughts – even the very strong ones – fell out of the sky, dissipated and died. I realised that thoughts need your engagement to survive, and if you could just sit back and observe them without engaging them, they had a very short shelf-life.

This part of me (of you) that is above and beyond, on top of and underneath thought is often referred to in spiritual texts as the I Am – the true self hidden behind the corpulent ego. What I have discovered and what I know is this: the I Am does not need lessons in thought control (it is the ego that tries to control thought and fails) because it is already the master of thought. This realisation, which came simply from observing nature, set me on a new path. Now instead of trying to control thought, I work on developing my I Am, that part of myself that already knows about thoughts.

This is done in two ways. First, lose the ego by renouncing comfort. This will allow the I Am to take its rightful place, centre stage. Second, sit in the dark and the quiet (dawn and dusk are ideal times) and allow the I Am to feed. This is where you nourish your true self.

I hope that this is not sounding too oblique or wishy-washy. For me this is real power. Nourishing your true self in the dark and the quiet is literally like a protein diet for the soul. It was a revelation for me. All I have to do is find quiet, sit in it and grow. This, too, takes practice. Many people struggle like mad to be quiet. They seek out noise. They can't even sit in the garden without the radio blaring. In fact for the majority of people there is not a room in the house (or an hour of the day) where the radio or the TV is not a constant and noisy backdrop. And that is because of ego. The ego knows that the true self grows in the quiet, and as the true self grows the ego becomes marginalised. Eventually, it fears, it will become extinct. So it fights like mad against nature, against quiet, against anything, in fact, that might nurture the self. This is why it is so attracted to addiction, because addiction adds layer upon layer upon layer on top of the self to block any thoroughfare for self-sustenance. And this is the main reason why beating addiction and finding quiet is so hard. The ego desperately wants to reign supreme and will fight tooth and nail to do so.

The irony is that the ego does not die; it just upgrades. It transcends to a new level, a higher level. Nothing can die. Everything evolves.

To develop the thought master (the I Am, the true self), kill addiction to weaken the ego, and nurture the self through meditation and quiet. The more you do this the quicker you will develop. As the self develops it widens like a net. I found that as I weakened ego and nurtured the self I was suddenly picking up ideas (for business, for health, for relationships) that I had never before even fathomed. It was very subtle at first. I found myself thinking more clearly, blocks of information periodically downloaded in my mind, as though I had somehow, in my meditation, made room for it. I was reading and finishing books (that would usually take me days) in an afternoon, and books that had made no sense before suddenly became as clear as spring water. I also found that I was attracting many, many more people into my life and business, as though they could somehow sense my expansion and wanted to be around it. I was getting phone calls out of the blue from people I had wanted or needed to meet. Uri Geller rang me one day, just to say hello. Interestingly, when I asked his advice about my path he simply said: 'Geoff, you need to expand.'

And so I did.

And the more I expanded the more ideas I was getting – ideas and information. And the more of that I got the more it encouraged me to want to expand again. I realised my potential to expand was infinite. It was I that set the boundaries. It was I that chose how high, how wide, how far, how deep I wanted to go.

And I found that the more darkness and quiet I can consistently give the self, the more it will grow.

All living things need sustenance. What we feed most lives and thrives most. What we feed least will atrophy. It is a universal law. What we pay attention to dominates. What we refuse to feed weakens and eventually dies.

This is true with everything, not least thoughts. So sit in your thoughts, cherry-pick the ones that you want to grow and nurture them. Take over the process manually at first. Undertake mental drills of healthy thinking until that thinking becomes habit.

There is an old story that I like. Two dogs are fighting in my head. One is black, one is white. The white one always wins because the white one is the only one I feed.

Which dog are you feeding?

As I said earlier, some people are not quite sure what it is in their life that is dark. They know that they have black dogs and they know that they have white dogs, but often they are not sure which is which. So let's have a look at that. Let's articulate exactly what darkness might mean to you and me.

Chapter 9

What Is Darkness?

First of all let's make one thing clear. Darkness is not the enemy. Darkness is the fertiliser for light. So do not try to escape darkness. Instead, embrace it.

The black is where light incubates. The deeper into the centre you go, the more propensity for the light to grow.

Back to the question. What is darkness?

Here are a few things that it can be:

♦ The wrong job.

♦ The wrong perception.

♦ The wrong caste (any caste that limits you is dark).

The wrong car.

The wrong house.

The wrong friends.

The wrong partner.

The wrong attitude.

The wrong life.

All wrongs are darkness, but all wrongs can lead to light. All! Even the densest energy can be transformed.

What is the wrong job, the wrong life etc? How do you know if it is wrong?

Before finding my path I worked in many jobs that made my days long and my depressions deep. These were jobs that allowed me to make a living, and for that I will always be grateful, but they were not jobs that allowed me to have a life. Not what I would call a free life. They were jobs where I learned skills, and I am grateful for that, too. But they were not jobs that I liked, certainly not jobs I loved, and many of them I truly despised. What is universally true of all the jobs I took on (and this is the greatest thing that they taught me) was that they were not my calling. Imagine this. You spend two-thirds of your waking life at work. Two-thirds. So you must make sure that your job is something that you love. Something that nourishes you. If it does not do that, perhaps it is time to change direction and seek out the job that holds true purpose for you.

Any job or life that does not encourage or promote growth is wrong for you because you are stifled. It will squeeze you in and smother you. It will stop your breath. And we all need to breathe.

Here's the paradox. The sad, dark feelings that your wrong job (or wrong anything) creates are not wrong. These feelings are telling you something vital. They are telling you that it is time to change. Ignoring these feelings, turning away from these feelings, walking away or running away or hiding away from these feelings, that is what is wrong.

We walk, run and hide away from these messages from the self, hoping to find help out there. But out there is just a mirror of what is in here. Eventually you run out of hiding places and are forced to listen. The feelings have all the answers. They lead to light. You can traverse the globe in search of a hide-out, trying to escape your dark, but you know even before you book the flights that such a place does not exist. How can you escape your self?

It is better to save time and money and go straight to destination you.

My biggest growth came to me when I was in my twenties. I had spent my whole life up until that point ignoring the messages that my dark existence was sending me. My marriage was volatile. My body sent messages telling me so. But people told me that marriage needed to be worked at, and that I was with the right girl, I just didn't know it. So I stayed. But my body kept crying out for change and kept sending me signs that said the opposite, but I learned to ignore them and quiet them and smother them. I tried to make something right out of something that was patently wrong.

My job in the factory made me feel very sad and unfulfilled. These sad feelings were my body saying: 'This is the wrong place for you. You can do better than this.' I asked my loved ones about it. Were my feelings right? They said: 'Be grateful for what you have, don't be greedy.' I asked my workmates the same question. They said I was lucky to have such a steady job, and warned me that jobs out there were scarce. They reminded me that I had responsibilities – a mortgage, kids, a wife. Why was I even thinking that I could do better, they asked? The intimation was that I risked their well-being if I even thought about leaving such a 'steady number'.

My ambition was trying to burst through. I wanted to follow art, I wanted to create, I wanted to write, I wanted to make films, I wanted to live. Those close to me suggested that I should not get above my station. I was made to feel ashamed for even thinking about a better life. The shame was enough to keep ambition in a small corner of my life.

Don't ignore the messages. Listen to the messages, and then do something about them.

Here is a list of examples of traps and dark places that you may recognise (anywhere you feel trapped, however, is darkness).

Violence

It is a dark existence when your life involves violence, whether physical, verbal or emotional. What I have learned and what I know about violence is this; it always rebounds on itself, no matter how well meaning you think it is. I spent ten years of my life being violent, and another ten years afterwards atoning. Whatever you give out will return. That is fact. You have probably heard that saying a million times. Maybe you are sick of hearing it. But I lived it. So I know it is real. If you take violence out of your arsenal, you will force yourself to find better and more productive means of problem-solving. Violence is a language, but it is the language of the ignorant and the scared. It is lower-echelon speak for the hard of thinking. I say think bigger.

What you attack will never go away. Like a boomerang it will keep returning until you realise that violence does not get rid of the problem. It might return wearing a different hat, a different face or a different uniform but it will keep coming back until you swap violence for a higher language. The best language to melt violence is love.

Grudge

Everyone that carries a proud grudge and brags, 'I will never forgive', literally chains themselves to their abuser. Grudge is a weighty anchor for the uninitiated and the ignorant. It not only keeps you in place and time, it keeps you in pain and anger. It kills your potential like a hammer to the head. The person who hurt you, who abused you, who did you harm yesterday, last week, last year or last decade will continue that abuse until you set yourself free by forgiving them. In the Bible, Romans 12:19 counsels us not to seek revenge for ourselves. Vengeance is the Lord's. Romans 12:20 continues: 'Therefore if thine enemy hunger, feed him; if he thirst, give him drink: for in so doing though shalt heap coals of fire on his head.'

Forgiveness is an act of great personal power that releases you from the karmic wheel and allows the universe (or God, or if you prefer – cause and effect) to repay the debt. Romans 12:20 tells us quite clearly that forgiveness is not 'letting people off'. It is not our job to 'let people off'. It is our duty to let ourselves off. Our abusers have their debt to pay and no one can prevent that. But you can set yourself free. By forgiving. As a doorman and a man of violence I used to revel in the grudges that I harboured. I would brag to people that: 'One day I'll pay them back. I have a long memory.' And many times I did pay them back, but in delivering the repayment I did not feel splendid. In fact it made me feel worse. It was as though my grudge tethered me to those I would repay, like I was some kind of pathetic puppet and my abusers were pulling the strings. When I got it, when it finally sunk in that power was not in holding on but rather in letting go, I cut the strings and I freed myself. And in freeing myself I sent my abusers into free-fall. Unable to suckle from me any longer, they were left to their own karma. And karma does not forget, not ever. The feeling of power when I learned to let go was and is immense. And I am in the business of dealing in power. That is my game. And whilst forgiveness often seems anti-intuitive, my life has taught me that it is the ultimate in power. If you are into revenge, if that is your game and you really want to get people back, forgiveness is (as Romans suggests) the ultimate revenge. It's like heaping coals of fire on your abuser's head.

To hold a grudge is to hold your own head over a flame. Courage is forgiving all debtors irrespective of the debt. What has been done to you is not of importance. All that is important is that you trust that the wheel of samsara (karma) will pick up and repay all. From my experience this is true. If you are not sure, try it. Be the proof.

Hate

An easy, salty, juicy emotion. Even the simpleton can hold and wield this gross emotion. But it is an emotion that – if left un-treated – will consume you. When you can take the emotion of hate (and let me tell you I have hated) from your belly and let it transform through your heart, then you are a true alchemist. You really can turn lead into gold. Let me give you an example.

I was watching the TV. It was Sunday and Sharon had cooked a little bit of dinner for us. The phone rang and even before I picked up the receiver I realised I had made a mistake. I like to switch the phone off on a Sunday, especially at dinner time. Eating is a solitary affair and digestion prefers peace and quiet if it is to do its job properly. Anyway, I made a mistake and I picked the phone up. It was an old friend from my past and his voice held the dullish texture of bad news. He'd been to the pub and, apparently, someone there – a nemesis from my past – had asked him to send me a message that he had some unfinished business with me. And the business was likely to get very bloody. My adrenaline kicked in, and my hate made its way to front of consciousness. I wanted to bin my dinner and beat a hasty path to the fellow's door to finish the said business before he made his way back into my life and finished it for me. But – mid-anger – I caught myself. I reminded myself that the feeling I was experiencing was just energy with a story attached (the story was a violent incident from my past that had not been resolved). That's it. It was just energy, and with that energy I could do whatever I wanted. I could marinate in it and pickle my internal organs with cortisol, adrenaline and noradrenaline (all very caustic), I could chase my loquacious friend and force the showdown, which might get one of us killed and would create more comebacks and more unfinished business either way (because with revenge there is no end), or I could be really wise and very courageous and realise two things. One – talk is cheap and pub-talk cheaper still. If this man had wanted a showdown, he would not have waited countless years for it. He was just a man with a (large) belly full of drink and a loose vocabulary. He was one man of many that line the bar of public houses and talk the talk. Two – this energy was very potent. If I could captain myself I could make gold from it. And that I did. I sat down, wrote the anger into a wordy article and sold it to a magazine. They paid me £400 for it.

I would like to tell you that anger is a negative emotion but actually it is not. The negative emotion part is just the story. If you kill the story you are left with energy that you can use to create something.

Lance Armstrong was a very angry man. He has courageously overcome massive cancer against all odds and has gone on to win the Tour de France an unprecedented eight times. But for his critics this was not enough. They felt that to win that many times, pretty much obliterating all competition en route, he must – he simply must – have been cheating. So they wrote about him. And they wrote about him. And they wrote about him some more. And let me tell you that in all their writing they had nothing nice to say about Lance. It was a pure, unadulterated attack. The politics of this were not important. What was important was Lance Armstrong's anger. What do you do when it seems as though the world is against you and this is creating so much anger inside you that you feel you might burst? Let me tell you what (clever) Lance Armstrong did. He knows enough to understand that anger that does not find a behavioural outlet is not good for your health. And as a man who had just overcome cancer, health was a burning issue for him. He also knew that blowing his top was not an option because his accusers were many. Chasing each one down would not be cost-effective. He would end up spending his whole life running after other people and not getting anything done. And even if he did chase them and did allow his anger out, this would only have fuelled the fire. Those journalists would have written more, and the abuse would have doubled and tripled in vitriol. A none too profitable endeavour, I think you would agree. What he did instead was get copies of every piece of criticism he could find, and just before his race he read them all. With the anger bubbling and growing inside him, he got on his bike and he raced. He used the anger as fuel. He became an alchemist. And he won race after race after race.

The enlightened few simply do not allow anger a resting place in their bodies. They simply take the high road. They realise that anger is an emotion of the ego, and to indulge in anger is to feed the ego. So they refuse to accept it, and because they refuse to accept it, the emotion goes back to sender.

I had a guy many years ago who hated me. He hated me with a vengeance and I never really figured out why. I don't think he did either, but it did not stop him from writing about me in magazines and insulting me in the written word. At first I felt a lot of anger, you might say justified anger, but to me it was just anger that was eating me up. I spoke with my friend Peter (a mentor). I asked him what he thought I should do. The abuse was getting more frequent and more aggressive. He knew the fellow who was criticising me and suggested that the best means of defence against his flaccid ego was indifference. I should pretend that he did not exist. Ignore everything as though I was a huge, important caravan moving purposely across the desert and he was a small, barking dog. It worked. The dog barked, but the caravan moved on. And the more I ignored him the angrier and more vitriolic he became, until in the end I was laughing at his childish attacks and he was seething with anger.

And let me tell you what the bestselling poet and magazine magnate Felix Dennis did with his anger. In a 1971 court case where Felix stood trial (with the two other founders of Oz magazine) for breaching obscenity laws, the judge said that Felix was 'very much less intelligent' than the other two accused men. Felix Dennis took this slight to his character (and the anger it created in him) and used it to deliver the judge perhaps the ultimate riposte: he built a publishing empire that is estimated to be worth £720 million.

Now that is what I call alchemy.

Jealousy

Dark and dense is the state of a jealous mind. We fear to trust, we fear to lose, we fear abandonment. We fear betrayal: actually, we fear everything. I have to tell you that I have spent some time smouldering in this emotion. And it was a dark place indeed. At one time I remember being so scared of a partner betraying me that I feared to have her out of my sight. It was pathological. Even if she was in the other room I was afraid that she might ring someone and betray my trust. Of course it is well known that jealousy is about low self-esteem, but that does not even for one second convey the sheer agony of a jealous mind. There seems to be no sanctuary from it. My fear of being abandoned was so intense that it felt as bad to me as climbing out of a dugout with a bayonet to attack an undefined but murderous horde. In the early days of my jealous suffering I tried to trace back to the roots of my insecurity. I found lots of likely villains from my past who had neglected me as a baby, abused me as a boy and let me down as a teenager. But to be truthful, whilst it was an interesting study, it did not solve my problem. What solved my problem was owning it. That is how I got through. You've got to own it. The issue was mine; it was not anyone else's. It was not my partner's fault. It was not that people could not be trusted. It was not my parents' fault. The issue was mine and I vowed to overcome it. On recognising this I told my partner how sorry I was for my needy behaviour and told her that I intended (not hoped, or prayed, or wished, but intended) to get past it.

Mine was a two-pronged assault. Firstly, I built up my self-esteem. I did this by actually looking at what I feared (in this case, abandonment) and then faced it. Abandonment was the story, and jealousy was the energy that the story produced. I killed the story and sat in the energy. I recognised that if I did not entertain the story (my lover might do this, she might do that, she might see him or her or them) the energy of jealousy could not be fed. And if it was not fed it would eventually die. Secondly, I exposed myself to the things I feared might happen. If I felt insecure when my partner went out alone, then I encouraged her to do that more. Rather than insisting I accompany her, I was adamant that she went alone. As well as gaining familiarity with the feelings that were trapping me (and ultimately trapping her), I also built my self-esteem by facing my fears. And I disproved the story by showing that what I feared was not likely to happen, and even if it did, I could handle it. The story was that my partner would meet someone else if she went anywhere without me. But by facing the fear I exposed the lie. Every time my partner went out alone and came home to me the story weakened, until in the end the story disappeared. I even started looking beyond the story and setting up new stories. I told myself that I was a great partner (at first I had to lie to myself – the fearful part of me didn't believe I was – but, eventually, after many such lies, I believed it) and she would be crazy to leave me. And anyhow, I told myself, in the very unlikely event that she ever did leave me, I would not only handle it, I would thrive in it. It would mean that I was a free agent and that I could go and live in New York for a year, or Japan or… You get the picture.

Jealousy is energy that is fed by a story. Use the energy for something positive until you can kill the story. Let go. What you let go of completely, you get to own. I realised a long time ago that the only things I could ever truly own were the things I could be brave enough to let go of. What you grip will perpetually slip through your fingers.

Envy

Envy is another easy emotion to buy into. Although I have never been a naturally envious person, I do know that it is a dark place for many. As you become more successful in life, the envious will turn an unsightly shade of green and slither out of the woodwork. That is a given. Any success will elicit this.

One of my students who lived in a very poor and undeveloped part of our city rang me one evening. He was troubled, which surprised me because less than a week before he was blessed enough to have won £5000 on the lottery. Not a huge amount of money, but in his deprived area enough to turn the neighbours green with envy. The gist of his concern was this: news of his win on the lottery had swept through the small neighbourhood and people were (believe it or not) very unhappy, to the point that it was causing my friend and his family strife. He'd had hate mail. His wife was being ignored by friends at the shops and even family members were peeved that some of his fortunate windfall had not found its way into their pockets. As I said, it was a relatively small amount of money, but enough to create far more problems than opportunities for them. He wanted my advice. What should he do? I told him to have a chat with his lovely wife. I recommended she go down to the shops and corner the neighbourhood gossip. She should then let the gossip know how sad they all were because the five grand that they thought might change their lives was all gone, wasted, squandered and lost. The next morning she did just that. Almost instantly the abuse stopped.

Although it is at a very low level of consciousness, envy is a very common energy that sits just below the surface in the majority of people, always looking for a reason to come out. It is there with most people, but like all energies it needs a story to exist. So in the instance of my friend I simply advised them to take away the lottery story (this was the story feeding the local envy) and replace it with another story: one of squander and waste. This story placed my friends safely back into the neighbourhood norm.

Rafe Esquith is a fifth-grade teacher of exceptional worth living in America. He has won numerous awards for his innovation in the classroom, from National Teacher of the Year to Oprah Winfrey's Use Your Life Award. Whilst the awards brought him fame and notoriety, they also brought massive envy on a scale that he did not think existed. And let's be clear here, he won the awards for helping children in underprivileged areas in America. This is a very altruistic and beautiful man. And yet, after winning the Walt Disney American Teacher Award, people from far and wide showed their weak and envious character by sending him hate mail and death threats. They left nasty notes on his windscreen and even wrecked his car. This is the power of envy when it is unrestrained. I personally would look at a teacher of this calibre and feel massively inspired; his success would fuel my own ambitions to succeed. During this violent time Rafe was very tempted to throw in the towel and let other people's envy end his illustrious career as a teacher. But he didn't. After much soul-searching he decided to use the envy of other people and the crucible of his own growth. He recognised that the fear and doubt their envy created in him could be – with effort – transmuted into something not just positive but profound. He used the weak character of others to develop his own character. He used their lack of integrity to build his own integrity into a tempered blade. And he did this by simply taking his consciousness to a level above his abusers. He decided that, no matter how bad the abuse got, he was going to carry on teaching. No matter how loud his detractors became, he would continue on. No matter how scared he felt, he would never give in. This built his character; it tempered his integrity and best of all it became a Sermon on the Mount for his students. By carrying on, despite it all, he became an embodiment of his teaching. So when he said to the kids, 'You can achieve anything', they knew it was true because their teacher was out there doing it.

What I do with myself if I ever feel envy is that I never allow a story to begin. If I feel even a smidgen of envy when someone experiences a success I immediately neutralise it by contacting that person and congratulating them. And I make the congratulations effusive enough to drown any feelings of envy I might hold. I also change the story in my head. I tell myself two things. One, if I harbour this feeling it will make me ill (it is a very caustic cocktail), and I simply will not allow that to happen. Two, I use the success of the person concerned as a reference point. If they can be successful that means that I can also be successful. If they can do it, I can do it. Their success can lead to my success, and my success is everyone's success. There is nothing that your neighbour has achieved that you cannot also access, and there is nothing that you have achieved that they cannot readily turn their hand to as well.

This is what I have learned and this is what I know: envy is a sign that we are not listening to our own intuition. It is a sign that, at some level, we feel that we cannot achieve what others have achieved. And if we harbour this caustic emotion it might well end up becoming true. Envy is such a potent energy that if we give it house space there is a real danger that it will push the success we seek away from us. It will push the people that can help us to succeed away from us. It has a negative effect on everything in your orbit. Let's be frank here: it is a pretty ugly emotion to place in your shop front. It tends to come, like fear (and it is a form of fear), wearing many different disguises. When we see people succeeding and complain that their success was not deserved, this is envy. When we accuse people of 'getting above themselves', this is envy. When we revel in their defeats, this is envy congratulating itself on being validated. When we cannot revel in other people's successes, when we cannot congratulate them, when we cannot celebrate them, when we cannot model them, this is all envy. Envy is below you and it is below me. It is the trait of a weak character; in fact, it is a force that grows weak character. Envy can be easily dissolved through congratulations. Congratulate the success of others until all you feel is inspiration. What you envy in others is what you doubt in yourself. Doubt nothing. When others succeed it allows us all to succeed.

Greed

The Upanishads, one of the most ancient texts in the world, says that, "Out of abundance they took abundance, and still abundance remained."

Greed comes from the belief that there is not enough. The scarcity mentality. When I was growing up in a normal working-class household in a normal working-class environment, this notion (that there is never enough) was drilled into me on a very regular basis, if not at home then certainly at school, and if not at school then definitely in the workplace. Statements like, 'Don't be greedy', 'I am not made of money', 'Who do you think I am, Rothschild?', 'Be grateful for what you've got', 'Money doesn't grow on trees', 'I've got to make this money stretch' and 'We need to save some money for a rainy day' plagued me. I am sure you have heard it all a million times. I know I did. And what it does is leave you with the firm belief that there is not enough of anything to go around. This becomes our truth. And as adults we carry it forward. We think there is not enough, we say there is not enough and consequently there is never enough. What I have found is that we create in the world what our truth dictates. We create poverty by thinking poverty. We create bad luck by thinking bad luck. I stood at the counter of a coffee shop one morning and listened to one of the elderly workers there, obviously close to retirement, telling his friend how unlucky he was, how he had always been unlucky, how he was just one of those very unlucky people, how luck was never on his side, and how when God gave out luck he was at the back of the queue. Within about two minutes this fellow had told his mate and everyone else in earshot, probably about ten times, just how unlucky he was. And that is why he was so unlucky. Because it is his truth. And his reality is projected from that truth. So he will always be unlucky. And in the unlikely event that he does win something he will probably lose it very quickly and very tragically, because he is so unlucky. Change the record!

I am very careful about the thoughts I engage in my mind. I am ever mindful of the words that leave my lips. I am as careful in my thoughts and actions as a man walking over a frozen lake, because thoughts that are invested with emotion become words, and words always want to realise themselves as deeds, and deeds are the final manifestation of an emotive thought. This is fine if your thoughts are of a benevolent nature, but not so good if they are loaded with negativity and darkness. What you think emotively, you order from the catalogue. It will come to pass. So change the record, change the beliefs and deliberately think good things (even if, initially, you do not believe them). Greedy people think that there is not enough so they horde and they hold on and they hide their pittance under the bed in a biscuit tin. But this is going against nature, which insists that in order to have abundance we must always give abundance. It is a cyclical thing. A tree takes abundance from the earth, and it gives abundance out through its leaves. But in the process of taking that abundance and transferring it through the trunk and branches to the leaves, it has abundance. If you look at a tree there is never a point where abundance does not exist. Successful businesses are the same. In order to have abundance they must bring in revenue, have revenue and then give revenue out. The moment you stop giving out you begin the process of atrophy. You begin the beginning of death.

I have a friend of a friend who is very greedy and it has cost him his business. He would likely not think of himself as greedy, he would probably call himself an astute businessman. But there is astute and then there is greedy, and this man was definitely greedy (he was as tight as a fat kid's PE shirt). He charged top dollar (which is fine, because his product was top dollar) and he had top dollars in his business account, but he did not pay top dollar to his staff or his suppliers. In fact, if and when he could get away with it, he did not pay his suppliers at all. He would deliberately hold off payments for as long as possible in the hope that his suppliers might eventually give up trying, in which case he would not have to pay them at all. Certainly he would make it very difficult for his suppliers to get paid, to the extent that some of the smaller ones went out of business. The world of commerce is a small one, especially when you are a greedy glut and a poor payer. Eventually he went out of business himself. No one would supply him. Customers did not want to buy from him. In the end no one wanted to deal with him at all. Greed always eventually rebounds on itself.

How many people, at some time in their lives, have not felt greedy? I know that I have. I know that even now, as an enlightened person, it can still try to creep in. You fear sharing because deep down you fear poverty, but – as anti-intuitive as this might sound – the exact opposite is actually true: the more you give out the more you get back. There is enough. There is abundance. The more generous you are to others, the more generous they will be with you. By giving abundance to others you are actually orchestrating the abundance back towards yourself. So I'm with the Red Hot Chili Peppers who advise their fans to, 'Give it away, give it away, give it away now'.

Here is a short poem (that I love) by John Bunyon that demonstrates how it works.

> 'There was a man,
> they called him mad.
> The more he gave,
> the more he had.'

Lust

Lust is just desire without its leash. It is usually associated with the profligacy of the sexual act. It is pleasure in excess. And, like greed, it creates massive imbalance, internally and, consequently, externally.

As coincidence would have it I have just had an email from Richard, a very spiritually-astute friend who is struggling with sexual lust and pornography. Let me show you what I wrote to him in response to his request for advice, and what he wrote back to me after reading my words (this can be related to any lust).

Me: 'Porn! This is a common addiction, especially with men, and I have a message for you about it. Porn is one of the many things that feed the senses and the senses gorge the ego and the ego blocks the I Am, the true self. If you want to develop the I Am you need to exercise your resistance to porn and other sensory excesses. Porn is neither right nor wrong. It is not a moral or an ethical issue. It is just an ego feeder, an addiction that keeps the I Am in a foetal state. Until you get this sorted, you will not develop a strong I Am, no matter how much you meditate. If you can weaken ego by starving it of sensory excess, whilst at the same time feeding the self (the I Am) with meditation and acts of selflessness, your spirituality will grow rapidly.'

Richard: 'I feel highly aroused before watching porn. When I pay close attention to these feelings they are fairly unpleasant. I feel a very acute sense of lack and desperation. Whilst watching porn I notice that my moral choices are degraded and I start to think things I wouldn't normally think if I was not watching porn. I also feel that it was training me not to empathise with my partner's experience of sexuality. Whilst this has not influenced my relationships with women yet, I feel it certainly has the potential to make me a selfish and unloving sexual partner. After I watch porn I feel deflated, lethargic and out of connection with myself. I wonder, "What am I doing with my life?" Reflecting on this helps me to more clearly see that porn is not something I want in my life. The two things that are attractive to me are instinctual gratification (physical sensations, seeing naked women) and a small amount of a feeling of connection with someone. This last bit is sad to me. I'm being more social now, which is fulfilling the need for connection in a far more nourishing way.'

In the past, when I have given up lust in obvious (pornography) and more subtle forms (watching certain adverts on TV, checking out women in the street), I have found that I start to feel somehow non-sexual. I feel freedom from lust and a sense that my love relationship can deepen because it is not being 'pulled down' by intensely genitally-oriented sexual exchanges. I do not want to end up the kind of person who says something a friend of mine recently said to his girlfriend: 'I don't need porn anymore. I've got you now.' I was a bit dumb-struck when I heard him say that, not least because it reinforced my ideas about what I am doing to myself when I watch porn and strengthen my addiction. I also notice I feel a lot more confident (I literally feel taller) when I do not engage in obvious or subtle porn. When I remind myself of the downsides of pornography, as well as all the positives that come from not indulging in it, the choice seems very clear.

What kind of life do you want?

Is porn worth it?

No!

I think Richard's reply says it all. Lust is a gross limiter, no matter what form it comes in. Either place a limit on your desires (and know that this will curtail – if not kill – lust), or become a servant of them.

Lies

Oh what a tangled web we weave, when first we practise to deceive.

There have been periods in my life where I have been a liar. A liar of the first order. And lying taught me one vital lesson. Don't do it. It is a dark and cavernous hole that few can dig themselves out of. It is never worth it. Even one lie creates an infinite network of lies to support the original sin, each feeding off the other, each needing the other to survive. I once lied for three years about an affair that I was having .It grew and grew until it was a hideous growth that ended up killing a marriage, damaging my children, unsettling my parents and shattering my integrity to such an extent that it took years and years of rebuilding before I even trusted myself again. They say that the truth sets you free. From my experience it really does. But it takes a titan to not lie. Many of us think that we don't lie, but probably we do, even if it is subtle, even if it is something that we might not necessarily label as a lie. A guy who does not pay all his taxes, who puts some through the books, but not all, is a liar. If you told him that he'd probably be incensed. No one wants to be thought a liar. But if you don't pay your taxes then you are a liar. When you fill in the forms you lie about what you have earned, and when the tax man comes to do a check on your books you lie again. This is why I always, always, without exception place every bit of my earnings through the books. Because

I am not a liar and I do not lie. When your partner asks you a question and you are not completely honest, even if it is just so that you do not hurt their feelings, you lie. You become a liar. You don't want sex so you lie and say, 'I've got a headache'. You want to get out to the pub (as quickly as possible) so you tell your wife that her dress looks fine, even though it is hideous. You are lying. You forget (or just don't bother) to reply to an email, so you tell the sender, when you bump into them at some future date, that you didn't receive it. You lie about it rather than say, 'I didn't have time', or 'I couldn't be bothered', or 'Actually, I just don't like you very much'. It is so hard in the flurry of everyday life not to lie, and so easy in our busy schedules (where everyone wants a piece of you) to rationalise our lies, or to downright lie about our lies. Lying leads to lying, and lying chips away at a person's integrity until it is all but gone. When someone says to me, 'I would have got back to you but I didn't get your message', I find myself thinking: 'If you are going to lie about something as small as that, what are you going to be like with the big stuff?' And do I really want to work with people who are liars?' You have to be very careful about the small lies, because small lies are like small cancers – they can still kill you, especially if they go unchecked.

I remember reading about a guy (we'll call him Ben) who had just landed his dream job. His new boss came to his office to finalise the details. Whilst he was in the office, Ben's secretary took a call from an existing client who had been trying to get hold of Ben for several days: emails, phone calls, messages. Ben had returned none of them. When Ben's secretary (with the mute button pressed on the phone) informed him that 'It's Mr. X again. He's been trying for days.' Ben shook his head and said: 'Tell him I am out of the office.' She duly did, and Ben duly lost his dream job. If he was prepared to lie so easily in his current job, how big a liability, his new employer thought, might those lies become in his new position?

Why lie when the truth is enough? The truth will always set you free. Men of integrity will always be attracted to you when you tell the truth, and the base man will always avoid you. That, on its own, makes the truth a worthwhile goal.

Judgement

Remember this one thing and you will never judge again. Whatever you judge in others is what you see (and perhaps hate) in yourself. In psychology it is called 'reaction formation'. The art of attacking in others what we most dislike in ourselves.

Everyone that comes into your orbit is your teacher. They all have something to impart. Each is a projection that your true self sends out in order that you might see clearly your own strengths and your own weaknesses.

If you don't own this, if you do not acknowledge that your greatest judgements on others are your own biggest shortcomings, you will find only perpetual darkness.

I used to run a small group of students who met once a week, loved to train hard and loved to talk psychology. I called it my Thursday class. It was invitation only. I limited it to players of a high calibre, and places in the class were highly sought after. There was one man that really wanted to train with us. He was a former student, a nice enough chap, but one who had gone off the rails somewhere along the line and had become ill-fit for my tuition. I hadn't seen him for a year or so but he was about to come back into my life. He had heard all about the Thursday class, and he knew that the lads involved were elite and he wanted to be a part of it. The request came to me via one of my students. I have to admit that my heart sank. I'd tried hard with this guy over the years and had managed to get him to a good physical level, but he could not seem to grasp some of the higher-echelon stuff and, consequently, had made some dark life-choices that automatically excluded him from my orbit. He felt his choices were right. I felt that they were pretty dark, and getting darker. I did not want to be any part of it. I am embarrassed to say that I actually felt repulsed at even the mention of his name. Anyway, the request was denied. I didn't want him in the class. The other lads didn't want him in the class either, so he didn't get into the class. But he was not happy with my decision, so he asked again. He wanted to know why I didn't want him in. I told him the truth. This was an invitation-only class and he was not invited. He was not happy. But then neither was I, because I still felt this odd repulsion and I wanted to understand why. So when the request came in for a third time I sat down and went into my feelings. It was here that I realised why I felt so repulsed by him. It was because his worst traits (the things I disliked about him most: his life-choices) were all things that I, at one time or another, had either possessed or considered. For instance, he was heavily into sexual porn and I really disliked that about him, but only because I'd felt that same lure myself. And whilst I did not take the path he had chosen, I had at one time been sorely tempted. He was also into crime, and I hated that about him too. However I had been a minor criminal in my past, and he just triggered memories of who I used to be. He was also a man who was heavily into denial. Searching the annals of my mind I realised that I, too, had spent many years in that dark place. There was not one thing that he had done, and there was not one thing that I hated about him, that I was not capable of myself. And that is why he repulsed me so much. I was looking in the mirror, eye to eye with my darkest potential.

This man was not an enemy, he was a teacher.

So I sent the message back that he was welcome in my class. I was grateful for his (unintended) tuition. I also knew that the Thursday class was top-end, no-quarter-given fighting, and brutally-honest philosophy. In short I realised that if he came to the class he would find out exactly who he was, and if he was brave enough to do that then I had to be open enough to let him. He declined my invitation. Months later he left the city and I have never seen him since. I am still grateful to him.

Judgement (and all the other dark emotions we have looked at) is about reflection. What you judge is what you fear in yourself. Left untreated, feelings of judgement are dangerous because the archetypes inside us, which recognise themselves in others and instruct us via our repulsive feelings, want out. And if they are not allowed out they can and will cause internal havoc in the guise of illness and depression.

If you want power – I mean real power – defeat these trolls. And the onus is always on you. With this in mind I need to warn you about one single thing that could completely neuter you and leave you utterly powerless.

Blame!

Chapter 10

Blame

We need personal power to turn dark into light. Blame rapes all our power. If you take responsibility and stop using blame as your reason for failure, you will reclaim all your power. Once empowered you can use your body to create literal miracles.

Blame is for the weak of will. And blame weakens the will further every time you use it. It actually completely disengages the will when you blame, because you place the fault out there. When blame is out there, you lose all power over it. Here are a few of the weak blame-thoughts that I have either personally employed in my past (before I found the way), or have heard used.

My depression! It's my mum's fault. She suffered depression all her life, so it is her fault that I became depressed.

What this fallacy meant (when I believed it) was that I was destined to be trapped by my depression (I had even learned to call it 'mine'), and that depression would always be the reason why I did not succeed in my life. It would be easy for me to say: 'If it wasn't for my depression I might have made something of my life.' As a young man who was scared to move forward and prepared to use any and every excuse available for his failure to act, this was a great temptation. Blame was always within easy reach. Then I read about Ghandi and my life changed. He was a man with a glut of possible blames at his disposal, excuses he could employ for not succeeding in life. He was part of a minority group, he lived in India (in a deprived area), he was physically a very small man (who was he to make a difference?), he was extremely scared, he was addicted to sex, and although he was a trained lawyer, he was not a good lawyer (he hadn't won a case in two years). What chance did a seemingly insignificant man like Ghandi have to change anything? Even on a local level he felt impudent. But despite all these odds this anonymous gentleman made personal changes that developed him into a leader of himself, then later into a leader of a nation, with an estimated 300 million followers. Through the practice of personal austerity he developed an iron will, he lost his addictions to excess, freed himself from darkness (even losing his fear of death) and went on to peacefully bring the British Empire to its knees, finally winning independence for his country. I realised that if a small, unknown Asian man from a place called India could do all that from such an impoverished beginning, then I could certainly negotiate my own personal limitations to live a free life despite the fact that I suffered from depression.

And that is what I did. I stopped looking to my mum for blame, and started looking to her for inspiration. She had been blighted by depression from an early age, and yet had still managed to raise a great family and live a good life. I decided to go one better. I turned and faced the depressions that stalked me, I embraced them, and I used that latent energy as a driving force for all my endeavours. That dark place called depression taught me more about myself, about courage, about God and about my own potential than any other thing in my life. Depression can be used as a good excuse to not even try, or it can be utilised as a catalyst for great success.

It's society's fault. I love this because I hear it so often and it feels so lame and misguided. People blame society, but we are society. They blame politicians, but we vote the politicians in and we can vote them out again. Everyone is society. So if there is something wrong, change it. You have the power, you are the power. I know many people who blame society for their ills, but it is not intelligent thinking. It is usually just lazy people looking for a faceless blame. If it is society's fault, what does that mean? Who are they going to corner and chase down and confront about their problems? I often talk to a local lady when I have my morning walk. She has had a couple of massive heart attacks due to stress and when I speak to her I can see why. She is so angry about society. She blames what she would term the ills of society (hoodies, criminals, immigrants, layabouts and the unemployed) on the politicians. When she speaks you can almost hear the blame and the adrenaline scratching around her veins, you can almost see her chest tightening and you can easily envisage the race of her heart as she sits down with pen and paper to write yet another letter of vitriol to yet another 'faceless' politician (knowing before she even sends it that her words are wasted and her health threatened with every angry line). She is so very angry, and her blame has no end. But when I look at what I know of her life, I wonder where the gripe comes from. Is her life really that bad? Is society really that dark? She is walking freely in 300 acres of beautiful country park, she is well fed, she drives a nice car along roads that are well maintained, she lives in a fine house with a loving partner and she is self-employed in a country that allows freedom of speech. She has a wonderful life. A wonderful life that she wastes ranting about something that probably does not even exist. I think she sees society as a collective behemoth, some disembodied monster out there. She probably imagines that when she sends her letters of protest to the council they are personally received by a politician that represents her imagined monolith. In actuality, they probably arrive on the desk of a bored secretary who shuffles (yet another one of those) letters around from one person to the next until someone pens a diplomatic reply that sends the woman's blood pressure through the ceiling.

When I was young and stupid and wanted to grow my list of blames, I always thought that the government didn't look after the ordinary people, not realising that politicians themselves were ordinary people. I imagined that the conspiracy theorists were right, and that there were people in a room somewhere trying to make life hard 'for the likes of us'. Later, after much experience and the strong decision to take responsibility for my own square mile of earth, I realised that if I could sack blame and become a dedicated autodidact I could expand my experience of the world infinitely. There was absolutely nowhere that I could not go, nothing I could not do and no one that I could not become. How exciting to know that my destiny was in my hands, and that my success was not in the hands of others. It was a choice. All I had to do was make that choice.

I had a great chat with my friend (the actor) Colin Salmon, who starred in one of the films I wrote (*Clubbed*). We were talking on-set about the need to take responsibility for your own life. He told me about the time, as a young, angry guy, that he thought society had it in for him. His dad sat him down in the front room one day and said (something like): 'Listen Colin. Your life is your own affair. It is up to you. There is not a group of people sitting in a room trying to make life hard for Colin Salmon.'

I love that. It is so wise and so true.

It is not society's fault if we are not happy. It is our fault because we chose to blame someone else for something that is entirely our responsibility.

It is God's fault. I like this one, too. It is over-used, of course. I am surprised that it hasn't worn out it has been over-used that much. God is a good blame because He is not available to defend Himself. We blame God as though He is a person, sitting in the sky with mean eyes and a beard, looking down and wreaking havoc on our world. How many times have you heard someone angrily say: 'If there is a God, why does he let people suffer?' There is a God, of course, but I doubt that He is a man or a woman or a being that likes us to spin and toil because of our sins. I doubt there are even sins, just actions that bring consequences, causes and effects. I see God in every split log and under every turned stone. It is an omnipotent, omnipresent, omniscient Presence that permeates all things. It is the force of everything, everywhere and at all times. It is not a bigoted, vengeful demiurge intent on proving its rule. So to aim your blame at God when things go awry is the equivalent of primitive man shouting at the moon, or wailing at the sun. No one really knows the whys and wherefores of God. Sometimes shit happens and no one is quite sure why. It is not for us to know every reason for every thing. I have been blessed to have felt the Presence of God more than once, and whilst I do not for a second pretend to know or understand this power, I can tell you this: it is too big to understand. To know that there is too much to know, is to know everything I need to know. They say that you should never ask to know the mind of Buddha, because it is too vast and we are too small. Like a bulb that takes more electricity than its capacity, we would 'blow' if we were exposed to even a fraction of God's power. In 'Paradise Lost', Milton advised us thus:

> Solicit not thy thoughts with matters hid,
> Leave them to God above, him serve and fear;
> Of other creatures, as him pleases best,
> Wherever plac'd, let him dispose: joy thou
> In what he gives to thee, this Paradise
> And thy fair Eve; Heav'n is for thee too high

To know what passes there; be lowly wise:
Think only what concerns thee and thy being;

God (the higher self, the universe) is a beautiful energy to which we as a species have access, that we can channel and that we can employ. But like electricity, this power needs careful handling. If we misuse electricity and get a shock we don't shout and scream and holler and call electricity evil. We don't run around blaming electricity for the wrongs in the world. We accept electricity as a massive source of energy that needs to be respected. We even train electricians to handle it for us, so that we do not get injured or killed, so that every day we can enjoy the benefits that electricity offers. We are still a primitive species that wants (and is gifted with) free will. But when that free will is misused and we end up in dark places, we want to blame a God that would allow that to happen. I love God. I am aware of His presence all around me. I am patently aware of the fact that I am here to serve myself by serving others. God is an impersonal energy that will give us what we intend to have. What we need to do is learn to hone our intent, so that we don't keep intending (through very strong emotive thought) all the wrong stuff.

It's too easy to blame and once you start to blame, the blame never ends.

There is no conspiracy. Conspiracy theories are for the lost, the weak and the easily convinced.

Break free from limiting beliefs. They are all limiting beliefs that suggest you are limited. And if there was a conspiracy to keep the ordinary man or woman down, how come so many very ordinary men and women have been so successful?

Prove to yourself that there is no conspiracy by setting yourself free.

You don't need to play the lottery. You are the lottery. Money will not get you out of the dark. It might buy you a sports car or a big house but if you are in the dark, you are in the dark, and everything else is just ornament.

If you think coin is freedom then the sooner you get rich the better. Once you get it, you can transcend it.

Freedom and light is knowing how to convert the dark. Once you know this, the car and the house (the 10,000 things) can be enjoyed as just one of the many things you experience and enjoy on this brief sojourn.

All you need to do now is make a list of dark things in your own life that are perfect for conversion. The first step to conversion is understanding. Knowledge can dispel fear (if not completely, then certainly enough to weaken it) so that we are better able to take it on and transcend it.

Chapter 11

One Fear, Many Hats

As I stated earlier, we think that there are many fears, but in fact there is only one. It is the fear of fear itself. All fears realised lead to the same place: feelings. As long as we are afraid of the feelings there will always be a pantomime of characters and situations that will happily dress up as that baddie Fear and step onto the stage of our world. We convert fear into light by first recognising this sage truth: at the back of all fears is one fear, and that is the only one you need to master. Until that realisation sets in and becomes your truth (because whilst fear is a master of disguise, it is also a master of deception, and will trick you again and again into thinking that is has many faces), it is best, from my experience, to line up the fears and take them on.

Here are some examples of the fears we harbour that are ripe for conversion:

Fear of criticism

Fear of loss

Fear of gain

Fear of pretension

Fear of rejection

Fear of death

Fear of criticism

The fear of criticism, if left untreated, can be a scourge. It can wreck your career, it can damage your life and it can retire you from purpose. The great novelist J. D. Salinger wrote a classic book called *The Catcher in the Rye*. The critics revered both the book and the author, who shot to global fame in the blink of an eye. His second novel, however, was not so well received. In fact, the critics despised it. Where with *The Catcher in the Rye* they had lionised Salinger, on his second novel they crucified him. He took it so badly that he has never, to this day, released another book. Not a single one. This is not because of the criticism; rather it is because of his reaction to the criticism.

We all want to be liked (I think I can assume that), we all want people to like our work, but the moment we allow their opinion to affect us to the extent that we can no longer do our work, we are in dire trouble. When I wrote my very first published article for a martial arts magazine called *Terry O'Neill's Fighting Arts International*, I got quite a bit of notice (on a local level, granted, but notice all the same). Some people loved the piece, and others thought: 'Who the fuck does he think he is?' I mentioned to Terry (the editor of the magazine): 'I've had a bit of stick about that article.' He said: 'Geoff, if you worry about what other people think you will never do anything.' I have remembered that piece of sage advice ever since. I know of one man (a champion carp fisherman) who became suicidal because he was criticised for (supposedly) using illegal bait in a contest. I know what you are thinking: 'It's just carp fishing!' But obviously, this man had allowed his hobby to become much more, and in doing so opened himself up to attack. Over the years I have been exposed to some severe criticism for my work, especially in the martial arts where I was always rocking the boat with my pioneering truisms. At the time I hated it. I wanted to kill someone. Later, retrospect showed me that the criticism I received tempered me. It made me very strong. So much so that in the end I courted it. I deliberately placed provocative work into the public domain that I knew would polarise people, just so that I could get exposure to my fears. And it worked. Let us be clear about one thing: when it comes to criticism, we are none of us innocent.

I said to my wife once, when I was receiving some heavy critique: 'I can't stand these critics.' She said something that completely changed my perception. She said: 'Geoff, we are all critics!' Everyone has something to say about someone or something that is critical. If you go to watch a film at the cinema and a friend asks: 'What was the film like?' You tell them, right? You say you liked it, you loved it, it was the best film ever, or you didn't like it, you hated it, it was the worst film in the world. The moment you offer an opinion, you become a critic. OK, some people are more public than others; some people use a newspaper to share their criticisms with the nation. But no matter the size of the audience, we are all critics. And not all criticism is bad; often it is good, even gushing.

Somehow, just knowing that we are all critics – all of us – helps to convert the dark (often debilitating) fear of criticism into light. Knowing that we are all just as bad as everyone else, and we are all just as good as everyone else, helps to humanise what is often an over-inflated issue. So someone doesn't like you, your work, your look, your opinion. Welcome to planet Earth. Welcome to the wonderful world of the individual. If you are not receiving any criticism, then I say: 'Get out more.' I pride myself on being an individual, I walk my own path. And you know what? Individuals get the most stick. Those that walk their own path get pointed at and whispered about more than anyone else. And also, know this: a person's critique just serves to lay their own selves bare. What they say about you will tell you a lot more about them. Their critique of you is an indication that they are not even meeting their own standards. And are you really going to take criticism from someone who beats himself up three times an hour?

Fear of criticism is just fear in a different hat. To get used to criticism, court so much of it that in the end it becomes little more than garrulous wallpaper. Let the dogs bark, but let the caravan move on. And if you hate it so much, stop being a critic yourself, because what you give out will return.

Fear of loss

There is no growth without risk. Really. People baulk at adventure because they fear loss. But without risk, adventure is no longer adventure, it's a guided coach trip. People fail to take on new opportunities, because they fear to let go of old positions. In order to cross a river, you must give up your footing on one stone to place your foot on to the next. To gain you must not only risk loss, you must also experience loss. For me to become a better martial artist I had to continually place myself at the bottom of someone else's class. To do that I had to experience the loss of comfort that being at the top of my old class offered. When Sharon and I first started our business we ran it from home, which at the time was a lovely, comfortable (tiny and cramped) house. To grow the business, and in turn to grow ourselves, we had to let go of that house and move to a bigger house. We loved that little place, and we felt sad at its loss, but to grow we had to put ourselves in a bigger bowl. We moved into a large and splendid detached abode (that we felt we could not really afford at the time) and within three years our business tripled. We went from eleven products to thirty in the space of three years. Without loss we could not have experienced that gain. And of course there was risk and fear in the move.

We risked not being able to make the mortgage, and losing the business. But we felt that this was down to us. If we decided that the move would be a success, then it would be a success. To experience abundance, first create a lot of space. Create a void, make massive space for massive expansion. For a tree to grow it has to give away (the loss) everything it has through its leaves. In giving everything away it literally creates demand for more volume, and the more volume it takes, the more it grows. And the more it grows, the more volume it demands (and so on), until the acorn becomes the oak. For new skin to grow, old skin has to die. In order to expand a snake must shed its old skin to make room for its new skin. Life is about loss, but in a very positive way. What I have learned to do is to court loss, rather than live in fear of it. I don't take stupid risks. I make all my risks as calculated as I can. It takes courage, but growing courage (I have found) is the same as growing anything: if you create the space for courage to expand by placing yourself in a void (where more courage is demanded), that courage will fill that void. It is called supply and demand. Placing yourself in a position of lack will encourage growth. I'd love it to work the other way around but it doesn't seem to. I'd love to say: 'Give me the courage and I will take on the fight. Give me the money and I will grow my business. Give me the muscles and I will grow my physique,' but we all know that it doesn't work like that. If you ask for courage you will find yourself in a difficult place that will demand courage, and then you will grow your courage. If you go to a gym and ask the trainer to build you a physique, he will put you on a high-protein diet and give you a set of heavy weights to move around. If you want a medal for running a marathon, then the best way to get one is to run a marathon.

I have a friend who desperately wanted to leave his job as a toilet cleaner. His long-term aim was to teach himself sculpting and make his living by selling his work. But from where he was this seemed a leap of faith too far, so he (eventually after much deliberation and fear) left his job as a cleaner and started his own T-shirt printing company. He was very scared; his greatest fear was leaving the 'steady job'. Even though he hated cleaning toilets, he felt safe there. He knew the mortgage and the car payments were covered. If he bought his own print company and it didn't work, he might lose it all. He eventually made the jump and, frightened of failing, he worked doubly hard to make it pay. He designed T-shirts with dog logos on the front, went to dog shows and sold them to people that loved all things dog. It really worked. It made him enough money to build an attic room in his terraced home, where he built a studio to develop his sculpting. It wasn't long before his sculpting work was starting to overtake his printing business and he was back in a familiar position. He could not develop any further as a sculptor whilst he was spending so many hours at the printing shop. So he delegated the print work out to his family, which allowed him more time at the studio. Eventually, after selling some more of his sculptures and finding his confidence, he took the leap of faith to sell the printing set-up and move full-time into sculpting, where he now enjoys an international reputation. I'd like to tell you that the decision to leave the printing and immerse himself fully into sculpting was easy, but of course it was far from that. He faced the same issues there as he did when he left the cleaning for the print shop. He had a mortgage on the house (which was a lot bigger now, due to the extension), and he also had a child to consider. So leaving the print shop, which had become a good, steady income, felt very risky. But what he did have this time that he did not have when he left the cleaning job was a very strong reference point. He had done it before, and it had worked. And with that in mind he took the chance and has never looked back.

If you are looking to grow without the threat of loss, or without the inevitable loss, you will look forever. Accept loss as a part of growth and you will expand beyond all your dreams.

Fear of gain

It might sound odd, but my fear has never really been about failure, it has always been about success. I can see my potential so clearly that it often scares the brown stuff out of me. Let me tell you about two of my darkest moments, both of which occurred on the cusp of great success. I can remember sitting on the train in London, about to embark on a country-wide, thirty-two-city tour for my book *Watch My Back*. You might think that this would be the happiest day of my life. A book that I'd written was on *The Sunday Times* bestseller list, and I was about to travel the country to promote it (me – the kid from Coventry who left school with no O-levels, the lad who pushed a broom in the factory for years and worked as a bouncer in nightclubs where people tried to marry my mush with a broken glass on a regular basis).

The opposite was true.

My success, or the weight of it, felt as though it were about to crush me. As I sat on the train, schedule in hand, a wave of anxiety and depression ran through me as I thought about the months of travelling, public speaking and staying in hotels that lay ahead of me. This little scared voice in the back of my head said: 'What the fuck have you got us into?'

Some years later I sat pickling in the same fear. I was in a front-row seat in a cinema at BAFTA in London with an audience of black-tied investors watching the very first public screening of my feature film *Clubbed* (inspired by my life). All I wanted to do was get up and get out of there. I was so nervous. It actually took all of my will power to keep me in my seat, and I do not say that in any kind of metaphorical sense. I literally wanted to run away. People were shaking my hand: 'What an amazing achievement. You must be so excited.' Actually, excitement did not even come into it. Unadulterated terror was closer to the mark. My fear was manifold, but perching vulture-like at the front of my consciousness was: 'What if it doesn't work? What if the film stinks?'

I am a man of experience, so I do know about fear. I know about its many disguises. It doesn't mean that I no longer feel fear, but it does mean that I am no longer tricked by fear (not for very long anyways). So on the train, pre-book tour, as well as in my BAFTA seat, pre-film, I turned to face the feelings and examined them. Because I did not panic, the feelings quickly dissipated. In the very darkest part of my fear, right at its centre, I found something very interesting. And it freed me. I found that my fear was not that the film or book would not work. I did not fear talking in public, and I did not fear sitting with an audience to watch a film that I had been working on for fifteen years. What I feared (again) was criticism. And I especially feared it from people I knew. When I went deeper still, into the blackest of the black where it became almost blue, I realised that my fear of criticism was really a fear of not being liked, not being good enough. My fear of not being good enough lead to the fear of being abandoned, and my fear of being abandoned was very primal. It was the ancient fear of being kicked out of the tribe. Being kicked out of the tribe is the equivalent of death. Millions of years of evolution kicked in, and my primal self was trying to protect me from death by trying to get me to take flight from the situation that had created my fear. But I knew that this fear was out-dated. It was no longer valid and, as real as it might have felt, it was actually a phantom, the residue of a by-gone age where abandonment (being kicked out of the tribe) literally did mean death. This fear was just old parts of myself (my archetypes) exciting a body where their tenancy had run out. The fear (in the Pythonian sense) was dead, deceased, no longer breathing (this parrot-fear is dead!). If my film failed and people hated it, life would go on. Next week it would all be forgotten and someone else would be on the end of the critic's nib. And if the book was panned and it didn't sell, I'd get over it. I'd try again. I'd try harder the next time. It would not be the end of the world because I would not let it be the end of the world. It would just be one more adventure in a life that had already been full to the brim, and that thought pleased me. Once I found this revelation (tucked away in the very black of my fear) I became excited. I realised that I was where I wanted to be, and that the best was yet to come.

The best way to overcome any fear is to be in its centre, where its power to damage is disconnected, and it's potential to transform is engaged.

In order to grow we need responsibility, we need success. Big shoulders are built by carrying heavy girders. They are not built by reading about lifting heavy girders. And wisdom does not come from a Christmas cracker, it comes from taking residency in dark places. We all know that we have infinite potential, and that is part of the problem. We all revel in our own potential, whilst secretly reeling in awe of our own possible success. But like the domesticated ox, your strength will grow in accordance to the weight you carry. And as you increase that weight, so your strength will grow.

Fear of pretension

I have lost count of the times I have found myself holding back in life for fear (that word again) of people thinking I am pretentious. Having come from a background of working-class people, I was weaned on knowing my place. Success (I was told) was not for the likes of us. Even the other kids at school bought into this fallacy and enforced it with each other. I remember coming home from my yearly summer holiday, a fortnight in Clacton-On-Sea, and telling my friends of the gorgeous girl I'd met at the seaside, and how I thought I might have a chance with her and… I was rudely interrupted by one of my mates (we were about 13 years of age at the time) who said: 'She wouldn't have anything to do with you. You're nothing special.' He killed my story with the sheer negativity of his words. 'You! You're nobody.' If the spoken word contained a toolbar, he'd just pressed bold, italics and underline (all together) on the words: 'You're nothing.'

When he said it, he definitely meant it. He pretty much spat it out. And I'm embarrassed to say that (out of fear of appearing pretentious) I totally agreed with him. 'Oh I know,' I said, apologising, 'all I meant was… ' and then did my best to find an early exit from a story that had suddenly lost all its flavour.

There seems to be a common belief that some things are just not possible for some people; that there is an 'us' and there is a 'them'. We should know our place, and stick to what we know. We should not get above our station.

A guy wrote to me (a fan, apparently) who'd read my first shot at a novel and had hated it. It had been a difficult book to write, not least because it was way out of my comfort zone. All my books up until that point had been non-fiction, an area I knew well and enjoyed writing. I was very sensitive about the novel (which, I am delighted to say, has now been adapted into a film script) because I had to shed an old skin to write it and my underbelly was exposed and vulnerable to attack. And this fellow did attack. His letter was a diatribe on how and why he despised my latest tome so much, concluding patronisingly with: 'Stick to what you know, Geoff.' This is what I was told as a floor sweeper. It is what I was advised as a hod carrier and then as a brick layer. It was what I was offered as a martial artist, then as a playwright and now as a writer of non-fiction who was venturing into fiction.

Stick to what you know!

I wondered what this what-you-know was that he wanted me to stick to. A month later, of course, I won a BAFTA for writing in a genre (film) to which I was very new, and in an area that I definitely didn't know. Suddenly, my 'fan' disappeared, never to be heard from again.

Let me state it here once and for all, just so that everyone knows how I feel, because I cannot be small and I will not be made small by people from small orbits. I may fall. I have faltered and I am sure I will stumble again, some time in the future, but I will never give up, and there is nothing I am not capable of if my intent is clear and my God is present. There is nothing that I cannot do, nowhere I cannot access and no one I cannot become. If I set my intention on it and open myself up to God, even mountains will get out of my way. I truly believe that nothing is beyond me or anyone else. If I set my intention on anything I am sure I could make it happen.

Who am I to be fabulous? Who the fuck am I not to be?

Why not me? Why not you?

All those fabulously successful people out there have two arms and two legs just like you and I. None are above us. None are below us. You and I simply know we can achieve anything. Where is the pretension in that?

Fear of rejection

I simply refuse to be rejected. In fact rejection can only happen if you expect to be accepted. If you don't care about being accepted, then you can never be rejected. So I refuse to need to be accepted. And I refuse to be rejected.

I watched a documentary on Bob Dylan once. It was shot at the height of his fame when he was being courted by the world's press. He was sitting in a car talking with a journalist from one of the top newspapers in the world, and you could tell by the pomposity of this particular writer that his stewardship at said rag was his raison d'être. He was also aware, and he made Dylan patently aware, that what he wrote had clout, and he could crush a man's career if he chose to do so. Dylan hated the establishment. He would not fall into line and try to justify himself, his music or his purpose as a human being just to satisfy the glut of this greedy behemoth. Climbing out of the car, angry at the journalist's bullying demeanour, he shouted back at him (something along the lines of): 'Write what you want. Ruin me. Do your best. I don't care. I refuse to be hurt.'

I love that. Love it. Dylan refused to be hurt. He refused to tow the line, he would not say what the journalist wanted to hear just to stay in favour. He did not bow down in awe of the mighty press. He did not recognise them, did not rate them, did not want or need them. He simply refused to acknowledge their power. In wanting and expecting nothing, he completely disempowered them.

Expect nothing from no one (but know that help will always come when you most need it and least expect it), then no one can hurt or reject you.

And, really, being honest, there is no such thing as rejection. It is just the erroneous perception that others own us, and in owning us they can reject us at will.

Take back your power and say goodbye to the fear of rejection.

Fear of death

First of all nothing can die. Science tells us as much, and intuition should confirm it. Life is perpetual. Nothing can really truly (in the full sense of the word) end. Everything is simply converted into everything else. It is the circle of life (as Elton John might have said). Every life form has a beginning, middle and a temporary conclusion. That's it. There is no mystery. We are a product of this spinning planet, and like every other life form residing here, we must at some point leave the corporeal state and transcend to the ethereal, or what is known as the next level. What is the next level? I have no idea, but I have felt it, sensed it and, innately, I know it, but do not have the wherewithal to articulate it on paper. Religions and mystics and philosophers since time began have tried to unravel the true mystery of death. They have all reported interesting ideas on life after death, but at the end of the day that is all they are: ideas. They may be right or they may be way off, but really it does not matter. Because no one seems to know conclusively (and many have gone mad in the perpetual fish bowl of trying to find out), we can assume that, at this point in our development, to know that there is too much to know is to know enough. Stop searching for the heavens and hells of the afterlife and start mastering the realities of the here and now. My suspicion is that if you master what is before you, you will open yourself up to more of what is ahead and what is around you. People are so busy trying to understand death that they do not take the time to understand and enjoy life. What I have learned and what I know is this; death is a daily affair. It is who and what we are and we need to stop fearing it. Death is a natural part of our everyday cycle. Cells are dying and renewing every second. And a new birth comes after every death. In fact birth of the new does not even exist without death of the old. Death is in everything. When we drink a glass of water we kill millions of micro organisms. Our immune system is killing things every second that we are alive, just to keep us alive. The killer T-cells in the immune system (small creatures with demonic horns on their heads) are constantly roaming the body looking for invading viruses that might threaten the organism. And when they find threat, the execution is savage: the viruses are horned to death. We kill things to stay alive. In fact we kill things to fuel our existence. Even walking to the shops involves the death of cells in the muscles, and the rebirth of new cells to replace the old. If we train, or work manually, parts of us die in the cause of that creative action. Brain cells are dying right now. The process of writing these words involves the expenditure of energy, and the energy expended is parts of me dying – dying for you, I hope you realise – to create this book. And, as is obvious, it is not really death, it is conversion; energy transcending into form. When we eat it is the same. The food is converted in the body to repair, grow, replace and, ultimately, to use as energy. The words on this page are the birth that is spawned by the death of expended energy. But, because all of this is largely unconscious, we do not see it as death. We just see it as hard work, a part of our everyday existence. On a bigger scale, the death of the whole organism (us), I would imagine, is no different. We presume that our own death will be sad, painful and a cause for mourning. Actually, it is just a part of the process. Nature (our own nature particularly) tells us that when this body expires we too will be converted, to transcend to the next great adventure.

I had had a brief look at death a few times as a nightclub doorman, and twice during periods of ill health. My flirtations suggested that death was an appointment that we all have to keep, and that the time was probably allotted in advance. One of the occasions happened during a choking fit when I could not breathe. Sharon was trying to Heimlich me, but to no avail. We had the obvious access to the telephone, we even had a doctor living next door, but there was an innate knowing at that moment that nothing, not a team of paramedics, nor a score of spiritual healers, could help me if this was indeed my time. Because my time would be my time and nothing short of divine intervention would be able to stop it. Once this realisation hit me (terrified me at the time) I suddenly was able to breathe again. It was as though I needed to see this truth before leaving my perplexed state of choking. Afterwards, reflecting on my experience, I was comforted in knowing that I need not fear my death because it would not come before its time. And when it's time came, I would be able to do nothing about it. I have read things that contradict this, but what I have read does not compare to what I have experienced. So I will stick to my own maps on this one.

The next time I had a close encounter with death was during a particularly difficult time of spiritual stretch. I was going through a dark night of the soul that seemed (to me) to last an eternity. I recognised, even amidst my pain and torment, that my discomfort was ultimately anabolic; it was a purification period that was a precursor to great spiritual growth. The Bible says that you cannot pour old wine into a new casket. The casket first needs to be prepared. My dark night was a period of preparation. I digress. It was during the middle of the night when I awoke. My body was doing frightening gymnastics against my will, things that I had not experienced so intensely before. My heart was racing, my body was shaking, I was sweating like a fat bird on a fun run, my head was all over the place and my throat was seizing up. In short, everything had gone haywire. Sharon – who is touch-sensitive to me – woke immediately and was very concerned at my physical state. I told her that I felt that I was dying. In retrospect, I can see that I was not dying. I was physically spent after a long period fighting internal demons, my physicality was stripped right back to the metal, almost at the point of collapse and this episode was just my body reacting to the state of my being. I got out of bed, sat in a meditative posture, calmed my terror, breathed very deeply and looked over my shoulder at death. I said: 'If this is it, then let me see you. I'm ready.' I must stipulate here that I was not being brave, I was not being a warrior. I was scared, I thought I might die. I tried to do what the Buddhists recommend when fear turns up at your door with all its hard mates. Face it. And this I duly did. In turning to face it I realised that this was (again) not my time, but if it ever was I was left in no doubt that nothing on this spinning earth could stop it. I remember feeling benevolence there. I had the feeling that Mr Death was actually Mr God, and that just beyond that shadowy veil was somewhere far better than my current abode.

And Sharon did what all sensible wives do when their husbands think that they are dying, she nipped downstairs and made me a hot Lemsip, which miraculously kept death at bay (the power of pharmaceuticals hey!)

Since then I have tried to have a more philosophical outlook on death and dying. I see it as inevitable (still scary), but ultimately exciting and definitely the big adventure. In order to live a brave life, the Samurai of old contemplated death every morning. After all, what is familiar to us often loses its sting.

But I think that, in this life, there are darker things than death, because death has its own schedule and we are not a privy to that. It is the more immediate shadows that we need to shed light on if we are to get to a new level of understanding. And some of these places are dark places indeed. But they are clever. They often creep into our lives disguised as pleasure, and once established in our daily habitual, they insidiously invade as a guest and end up becoming the host that, eventually, sets about wrecking the whole abode.

I call these invaders 'the big five'.

Chapter 12

The Big Five

There are some very dark places in this world that are the anathema of our species. I call them 'the big five'. If you want to see the terrorist of your world, your country, your city and your streets, stop looking for the obvious armoured invaders with back-packs and boot bombs. These are often just flash-bangs used to distract our attention away from the real threats. The jihad that we need to embrace is the only jihad that really exists: the internal war against the insidious invader.

It would be easy to look at the forthcoming list and see the big five as moral or ethical issues. I don't look at them as either. Rather they are actions we take as individuals that have consequences that can and do lead to the imprisonment, often the atrophy and sometimes even the death of the organism. So this is not me crusading for or against anything, I am just laying out information (the elixir of my warrior journey) that you can either heed or ignore. Your choice.

The big five:

1) Pornography

2) Drugs

3) Gambling

4) Junk food

5) People pleasing

Pornography

It is a dark place indeed that finds you locked in but claiming to be free. People say: 'It's not an addiction! I can take it or leave it.' And yet, when they try to escape, they often can't leave it and end up trapped in cells without walls.

If you think you are really free of addiction-prison, try to escape and see how your body and your brain react. Then you'll know. Watch how your jailer lures or frightens you back to your cell the very instant you try to open the door.

As I said, addiction is not about morals or ethics, it is about cause and effect. If the cause is excessive then the effect is often destruction or addiction, the prison without walls. With any addiction we are offered two choices. I recommend that you make the latter. You either choose to stay locked in your cell and stop complaining about it, or kill the addiction and escape. If you know the way out but choose, for whatever reason, not to take it, stop bitching about it because you have no right. It is very tiresome to hear people complain about circumstances that they can change but choose not to.

Addictions tend to find their way into our bodies via the senses. What is accessed strongly through the senses stays on the hard drive (hence the addiction). Only when the senses are starved of this negative stimuli will the virus be cleared.

Pornography (in all its disguises) excites the sympathetic nervous system, floods the body with adrenaline and cortisol and other caustic elements. The immune system closes down temporarily leaving the aroused highly vulnerable. When highly aroused we tend to go out of the body (that is, our rational self disappears and our addicted ego takes over). This is why we often feel as though we do things against our own will. When the master is not home, the house is open to all sorts of maleficent intruders.

Intuition, inspiration and art are absorbed through higher levels of consciousness. When the body is over or falsely aroused, levels of consciousness descend to a very base level, more in line with the profligate dog than the creative human being. An over-stimulated body cannot find enough behavioural escape for all the hormones released during arousal. The unused adrenaline roams the body looking for its war to fight. Finding no such battle, it either creates a displaced outlet (anger, road rage) that causes us untold conflict, or it becomes root-bound and starts attacking the smooth internal muscles, like the heart, the lungs and the intestines. It even travels to the brain and picks a scrap with neurotransmitters and brain cells. Not moral, not ethical, just biological: this is a matter of survival.

Excess kills more surely than a bullet to the head.

The issue with sexual porn is that it fools us into thinking that it is natural. Let's be honest here. It feels very nice, and (we think) it's not harming anyone. But it does harm. Sexual pornography ruins relationships. When men – dangerously stimulated – want frequent, profligate sex (often up to eight times a day), their partners just cannot cope. I know this from my own experience of exposing myself to porn. It leaves you with very twisted stereotypes of women and how they should behave during sexual interaction. And when the woman in your life does not correspond with the women in your mind's eye, it is the base for conflict. What I find disturbing is how quickly the pornographic images imprint themselves on the brain, and how hard it is to remove them once they are there. Like any addictive host, this one is insidious. It creeps in little by little until it is established in your head and you can no longer control it. Once established the host needs to be fed, and so you find yourself doing things completely out of character to feed it. But as I said, eroticism by its very nature is pleasure. Because of this we often fail to make the decision to kill the addiction. Like most addictions this one lures you in with loss-leaders that often arrive (uninvited) onto your computer screen or in your daily lad's mag or newspaper. The loss-leader wets the appetite, and sets up a Pavolovian arousal system that leaves us wanting more. And all we have to do to access more is to press 'enter'. Suddenly we are in an Aladdin's cave of salacious images that call us back again and again and again, until – at some point – we need stronger and stronger doses to get the same high. We might even allow it to spill into our everyday reality, and go hunting for it in the flesh.

It is your choice if you want to engage in this activity., but I feel that the choice does need to be informed. Rather than fall into the easy vat of ignorance and denial, at least get the basic cause and effect facts so that you can make an informed decision.

Drugs

Drugs don't kill us. Ignorance kills us. Weak wills kill us. Greed and laziness kill us. Self-pity kills us. Unearned pleasure and comfort kills us.

Drugs are just the delivery system.

People kid themselves that drugs do not harm, but history, statistics and intuition prove otherwise. People know drugs are killing them (it even says so on the packet) but they do not exercise their will to resist.

People are greedy and lazy. They want instant gratification at any cost (preferably at no cost). Ironically, people end up paying for their ephemeral highs with their life. This lust for easy pleasure often comes from the root of self-pity. Many people are self-pitying. Life is hard, they say. Why shouldn't they take relief in an artificial God?

Because it kills you, stupid!

Kill the self-pity. It is tiresome. Listen to the Buddha: life is difficult. So, stop bitching and get good at handling it. In fact, why not take on difficulty and become piss-excellent at handling it. There are better ways of getting high than with degenerative additives, ways that require applied courage, deliberate (anabolic) suffering and conscious labour. They bring the kind of high that separates you from the masses and allows you to channel essence of God.

The way to heighten pleasure and comfort is to earn pleasure and comfort through your own labour. The high you get from achievement, from excelling, from taking on the odds and resisting the senses is far better that any artificial high. And it does not come with the catabolic aftermath. How tasteless does food become when you don't work for it? How tepid is the tea that you have not earned a thirst for?

Someone once said to me: 'If that is the case, how come a blow job is always so nice?'

The level set by the question kind of negates the need for an answer.

Drugs are an easy lure, one for the sheep. Ironically, drugs kid people into thinking they are individuals because they buck society. But I have to tell you that society does not give a rat's arse. Society is too busy trying to get its own shit right to worry about anyone else's. If you want to be a real individual, a real stand-alone, don't fall for the honey trap, because it is set for fools. Being a fool is not the same as being an individual.

Alcohol

The curse of the working classes. The curse of the species. Actually alcohol does not kill. The greedy glut kills when he does not court moderation, or employs excess and labels it moderation.

I had a friend who ran pubs. I was talking to him about drugs. I was writing a film about a drug dealer and was telling my friend how my research had led me to a meet with one of the top dealers in the country. My friend's face twisted in repulsion. He said that he could never talk to a dirty, scumbag drug dealer. He'd have to report him to the police. He made the same mistake as many. He saw it as a moral issue, when it was more an issue of personal responsibility. And anyway, my friend had a mote in his eye. I told him: 'You deal drugs. You run two pubs. You sell alcohol, and alcohol is a drug that kills tens of thousands. It actually kills far more people than class A drugs.' He was taken aback. 'Alcohol is legal,' he said weakly. 'But it still slaughters tens of thousands of addicts,' I replied. 'Just because it is legal does not mean it's good for you.'

Cigarettes are legal, they kill thousands too. Alcohol is another one of those insidious addictions that takes over and becomes host in your body, but allows you to believe that you are in charge. By allowing you to think that you are still in charge, you are unlikely to ever challenge its occupancy. Alcohol is so good at pretending that it is not a threat that, even right up to the point that it kills you, it can still leave you feeling in control. One of my friends was a raving alcoholic and it was killing him. His family told him so, but what did they know? The doctors told him the same story, but everyone knows that doctors don't have any clue. Even after losing one of his kidneys to alcohol abuse he was still in denial. 'I can quit any time I like,' he claimed, believing that he was in charge of his habit. But he died anyway, still parching for a beer.

My brother was five days away from death before he (or we) could acknowledge that he had a problem. By the time he admitted it to himself his body had already buckled, and then it broke and we lost the most amazing man.

Alcohol did not kill my brother. Denial killed my brother.

When I look around me I see many alcoholics who do not see themselves as alcoholics, because their idea of an 'alchy' is some drop-out on a park bench having it large from a brown paper bag. Their denial does not change the facts. They can't stop. And if the habit has become the host, then no matter what you want to call it, you are an alcoholic. If you feel that you are not addicted, try and go without a drink for a year, or even try and go without a drink on your two-week holiday and see how your host hollers at even the suggestion.

Does this mean that alcohol cannot be drunk in moderation? No, of course not. There are some who can do it. But for every one person I know that is moderate, there are an uncountable number who claim moderation but drink in excess.

Gambling

It is legal, millions do it, so it must be OK. Right?

We are, it would seem, a nation of gamblers. The lottery is played by millions, and there are casinos opening every day in some part of the country. People want success on the luck of the draw because they are either too lazy to go out there and become their own lottery, or they don't believe they can acquire their fortune any other way. I don't believe that gambling is necessarily wrong, I just think that playing the odds and chancing luck to bring fortune is disengaging your own potential to excel. I know when I was in the factory, many of my co-workers felt that the lottery was the only way 'out of the rat race'. If you buy into lottery mania you are buying into this wrong and negative premise. I don't play the lottery for this reason. I don't want to win it. I intend to earn it. I do not want to jump in a helicopter and be placed at the summit of Everest without acclimatisation. I see myself as a mountaineer, and I see my peak as my goal and my responsibility. I intend to earn my spurs on the ascent, on the journey. The peak just represents a culmination of one journey. I personally do not want to win my marathon medal by picking a number out of a hat. I do not want an honorary PhD and I do not intend to win my fortune by picking numbers and hoping for the best.

As for habitual gamblers, they are no different from habitual drinkers; they always place their bones and the bones of those they love on every hand they play and every dice they throw. Like alcohol, this is a selfish act that sees addicts seeking pleasure that they know will cost their loved ones in pain. And there is no amount of money (as there is no amount of drink) that could satiate the gambler's lust. But if we are talking gambling, of course, we might as well be talking alcohol or porn because all addictions are one (like fear it just wears many disguises). Society promotes the gamble as fun and harmless on one hand, then attacks it as a vice and crime on the other.

I say: 'Fuck society.' You promote and you attack yourself. So stop.

Junk food

Junk food is the new cocaine. It is the opiate of the masses, only it kills more people than coke because not only does it promote excess but, by its very nature, it is excess. And excess in food leads to obesity, and obesity is the new plague. Again, denial is playing its part and protecting the addicted host from detection. But let's cut the bullshit. Let's level the denial and call obesity what it is: excess dressed as moderation. It is greed pretending to have 'big bones', creating bodies that over-pay themselves in food, then refuse to do the work. They eat like steel fixers without having the steel-fixer's workload. The solution is easy enough in principle, but difficult to put into practice: eat what you earn, eat what you make room for, what you need for fuel. Everything else is excess (or greed).

It is not common knowledge but at one stage of my journey I was three-stone overweight. I could hide it well because I am tall and muscular, but the bottom line was that I was carrying a lot of excess weight. I think this is commonly called fat! Like most people, I pretended that I was carrying my weight in all the right places, which worked until I looked in the mirror and saw that those 'right places' included my legs, my arse, my belly and my fat face. Being a fit person (I have always trained every day), I rationalised that whilst I was quite heavy (nearly sixteen stone), my body was 'functional'.

Now, 'functional' is a very good word to use when you don't want to say fat, obese, lardy, chubby or down-right greedy. I was excessive but pretended that I was moderate. Then I read a line in a book that changed the way I thought about things forever. We are often sceptical about the life-changing qualities of words, but these words changed me in a heart beat. The words said something that really struck home. They said (as though the author was speaking directly to me): 'You think that you can flirt with your addictions, but you can't. Either they are dead or they are still a threat.'

Whilst you allow them to live, whilst you continue to flirt with your destiny, you will always be in danger. Addictions are funny things, almost like small entities in themselves. They are patient, and they are always looking for a way in. Because once they are in they burrow, set-up residence and eventually take over. The moment I read this I took action and started to cull my addictions. Without mercy. One by one I struck them down. My main addiction at that time was food, specifically of the junk variety. And this is the interesting bit. The moment I decided to lose weight and shed the excess, I knew innately, without anyone having to tell me, exactly what I could and should and what I could not and should not eat. Even the portion sizes were obvious to me. Before this I had gone on myriad diets. I'd had friends (nutritional experts) write me out eating routines because (I thought) I didn't know what food was good and what food was not. This time (because my intent was definite), I did it all myself. And I lost three stone without really having to try. The point is, I knew what to do. When we are ready to kill an addiction, we all know how to do it. Each and every one of us. I'd love to give you a list of foods that are good for you and a list that are bad. I'd love to throw the gamut of healthy eating your way, but that would be patronising. You (me, all of us) already know what is good and what is bad, what is healthy and what is junk, what is moderation and what is excess. And if you genuinely feel you do not know, you should make it your business to learn, because your very life depends upon it.

People pleasing

People love to please people because they fear not to. People pleasing is another cell with invisible walls. Another dark place. Fear wearing yet another hat. If you worry about what other people think you will never do anything. At the back of people pleasing, feeding the habit, is low self-esteem. We want to be liked and we feel that if we say no to anyone they won't like us. So we say yes, and deep inside we hold dark resentments because we know that we should have said no. Ironically they are dark resentments that we fear to bring out because, again, people might not like us if they saw that side of our personality. This resentment that we hold inside can cause all types of illness. It is a rogue energy that roams the body, wreaking havoc because we will not let it out. Carl Jung called this energy the 'shadow self'. The shadow knows that for the health of the organism (you) it needs to find a behavioural release, but because of our people-pleasing tendencies there is no way that the conscious filter is going to let this happen. So it keeps it locked up. And what is suppressed will fester. People pleasing has always been one of my own personal demons. I am not sure where I learned it from – if I inherited it, or whether a past-life incident is at the root – but it's there and it has been very potent in my life, to the point that it has at times made my life a misery. I was always letting people take advantage of my inability to say no (especially strong women). I desperately did not want them to think that I was not a nice person, that I was mean or greedy or somehow not Christian. I am much better now because I work on it daily (my practice usually consists simply of saying no when yes is not appropriate). I have had to lose many people from my life because they were so used to pushing me around and forcing a yes out of me that when I suddenly started to say no, they could not cope with it. My inspiration came from the brilliant writer Sue Townsend who suffered the same difficulties. She was so afraid of saying no to people that it made her very ill, to the point that she was nearly blind, incontinent and wheelchair-bound. It was only as a virtual cripple that she could finally say to people: 'I'd love to say yes, but I am blind, incontinent and in a wheelchair, so I have to say no.'

I had to learn that wanting people to like me was an expectation. I was expecting something. To be really happy and successful I had to let go of that expectation. In fact, I had to let go of all expectation. The very act of placing your head above a parapet will win you enemies and friends in equal numbers. By the very nature of this ambiguous, multi-faith, opinionated life you are never going to please everyone. And the very act of trying to please everyone is the first step towards failure, because you no longer retain your own true sound. Yours becomes the voice that you think people want to hear, a voice that will have to change according to who you encounter. There is no individuality or integrity to be had there. Just sadness and the loss of self.

The irony is I thought that people might dislike me if I said no, but the opposite was true. They actually seemed to like me more, even respect me more. And those who did not like me for saying no, well, I don't want them in my life anyways. People pleasing is poison. The best way to stop it is to practise saying no. You don't have to be angry about it, you don't have to be rude or inappropriate and you certainly don't have to justify why you are saying no. Just say no and move on. It gets easier. The practice definitely makes for a light reality.

One of the places that taught me the art of saying no was a nightclub called Busters. I was working there as a bouncer in the late eighties. I had to say no to people on a nightly basis, and I had to live with the fact that many people would not like me, simply because of the job I was doing. It was a sobering time (see my book *Watch My Back*), a time of violent unrest in Coventry and a time that tempered me as a person, but not before I almost lost myself in the dark abyss that is violence.

Whilst people pleasing is a dark place to find yourself, I have to say that it was not so dark and not so dense as living a violent reality. If people pleasing is a muddy place, then violence is a pit of burning tar.

Chapter 13

Violence

Friedrich Nietzsche said that we should be careful when hunting the dragon that we don't become the dragon. I became a nightclub bouncer in my late twenties to overcome my debilitating fear of violent confrontation. But in my pursuit of courage I became extremely violent myself. The dragon that hunted the dragon definitely did become the dragon. But I eventually came out of the other end (otherwise I would not be here now, writing this book) and I learned some valuable lessons, not least that violence – even well intentioned – always bounces back on itself. The use of violence to stop violence (which, scarily, I once advocated) is futile. You don't get rid of black by adding black. Violence is the language of the ignorant. Using violence to solve violence is just the ignorant conversing with each other, only people get battered or people get killed during the discourse. So, learn a different language, a better language. There are many languages that are better than violence. Here are just a few that I learned during my decade of violence: avoidance, escape, verbal dissuasion, loop-holing, posturing, metaphysics, love.

Avoidance

Violence is a double-edged sword. There is the violence that is inflicted upon us by others, and then there is the violence that we inflict upon them. I have spent time in both camps and can categorically tell you that whilst I was living with a violent mentality, I always attracted violence towards me. And when I changed my mentality, when I stopped thinking about violence, I stopped being violent towards other people and I stopped experiencing violence that was aimed in my direction. I will go into that more in a later section of this chapter (Metaphysics). Before that I'd like to look at how you might immediately avoid violent people and violent situations in your everyday life.

Much of the violence reported in the media is environmental. This is not to say that violence has not escaped the reservation and bled across into nicer areas. Of course it has. Because of this we need to employ vigilance in the way we go about our business (for more on this see my book *Dead or Alive*, or read *Streetwise* by Peter Consterdine). But, generally, violence thrives in negative environments – the shit holes where arseholes hang out. So, avoid shit holes and arseholes (and don't be an arsehole yourself). If your environment is volatile, remember this: you choose your environment. So, choose better. Avoidance is about making yourself a hard target, and not placing yourself in harm's way. This might seem overly simple, it might even appear to some as a little paranoid, even patronising. But it is no different than what you would teach your children about road safety. You don't teach your kids about first aid just in case they get knocked over by a car, because you know that if they get knocked over first aid might be too little too late. If they get knocked over on the road the chances are they will be dead. So you teach them how to cross the road safely (remember the green cross code? Look left, look right, look left again, then cross) and pray that they heed your advice.

Avoidance is to self-defence what the green cross code is to road safety. It is a way of avoiding a tragic accident. From my experience of unsolicited violent assault, it always ends tragically for someone.

If you can't avoid (we are only human), then escape.

Escape

If you find yourself in a potentially violent situation and there is any chance whatsoever of avoiding a confrontation, do what nature tells you to do, escape. You have a million years of evolution in your genes urging you to run. So, help it to help you by listening. There is no room here for cares about how it will look, and whether or not running is a cowardly act, this is about survival, so if the situation allows or demands, run. Forget ego! Ego is just a fat pub-fighter that wants to defend its corpulence. And do not even entertain peer pressure – who cares what your mates think? When you're dead or maimed you won't be able to care. Avoid. If escape is not an option you could try....

Verbal dissuasion

Talk it down. Always, if you have the choice (and you usually do have the choice), use verbal dissuasion to convince the person who wants you to enter his darkness that fighting is for fools. It is best left to dur-brains and Neanderthals. From my experience of violence very few people really want to fight, they are usually just blowing off steam. If you have the fortitude to hold your ground and become a little loquacious there is a good chance that you can talk your way out of it. As a young, insecure doorman I always hit first. I was scared and my fear did not want to take any chances, so I lashed out and was violent in many situations that might have held a peaceable solution. As my confidence grew I was able to see that most of the people I faced were not really violent, they were just garrulous. So I learned to hold fire on the bombs and sent in my very confident, very beautiful inner negotiator, who was able to pow–wow a way out that did not involve an ambulance and a team of paramedics (followed by the police van that would take me away).

Part of verbal dissuasion is what I termed Loop–holing.

Loop-holing

To loop-hole is to give someone an honourable exit from a potentially violent altercation (a fight). As I said, most people do not really want to fight even if (often especially if) they say they do. So, all you have to do is give them a way out that is honourable (something that they can tell their mates). One way of doing that is to simply be honest and tell them that you don't want to fight, that way they can exit the affray and tell their mates that they let you off. You get to walk away, and it is only the ego that gets a spanking, but I figure he wants you in his perpetual darkness, so he needs a good spanking. As a doorman I used loop–holing prolifically. I would often tell people that we (me, the other doorman, the club) did not want trouble, and that we would appreciate it if they just walked away. Other times if I felt someone was going to be violent with another customer I would ask them not to kick-off as a personal favour to me. This would enable them to exit the situation (that they didn't really want to be in any way) and tell their mates: 'I'd have killed the bloke, but Geoff asked me not to, as a personal favour.' He knows it's bullshit, I know it's bullshit, secretly even his mates know it's bullshit, but it works, and it is a better, alternative language to violence and that is all that matters. Other times if I felt that a situation was about to become physical I might suggest that we postpone the fight, meet another day, perhaps for a drink, so that we could talk about it. The implication here again is that I do not want to fight, that I would rather talk. He can walk away knowing that he was not the one to back down first. It is all mostly working on male ego, which is always at the forefront of fights, especially after alcohol, but as long as it offers a loop–hole nothing is lost.

If your avoidance has been lapse and escape potential lost and verbal dissuasion or loop–holing has failed, posturing can be a very effective language in the avoidance of violence.

Posturing

Posturing is very simple. You just need to make like a mad man. Shout, scream, splay your arms (to make yourself look bigger) balloon (pace maniacally from left to right) salivate and use as many expletives as close together as you can. This (if done convincingly) will kick-start your aggressor's adrenaline (adrenal dump) and trigger the 'flight response'. This instinct is so strong that it will force the majority of people to run like the wind blows. Certainly only the veteran will walk through a practised posture into the physical arena. For the posture to work it needs to be very convincing. When you shout, it is important to place massive intent behind your voice. You are not shouting old ladies onto a bus. The shout needs to be primal, from your very boots, so that it triggers the fear of God into the person in front of you. He needs to feel as though you will kill him if he does not run away quickly. It doesn't even matter that you don't believe it, what matters is that he believes it. When ignorance is mutual, confidence is king. In showdowns like this it is the one that appears more confident that goes home with the trophy. So let it go. And make sure at all times that as you posture you maintain a safe gap between you and your antagonist. It is this gap (along with strong posturing) that will trigger his flight response. As soon as you can, use the gap created and the fear instilled to make your escape.

Although I have to say that, if you can practise good metaphysical self-defence all of these strategies will not be necessary, because you will not create the situation in the first place.

Metaphysical self-defence (MSD)

It is not the world out there that gets dark and light. It is our thoughts, acting upon the world, that create the hue.

When I was thirty years old all I thought about was violence. I thought about it, talked about it, read about it, watched it on video and dreamed about it (I even had a weapon in every room of my house, in case someone broke in and I needed an immediate appendage). And all of my thinking was emotive; so much so that my life was copiously brutal.

If violence was currency, I was a multi-millionaire.

Then one day it hit me. That eureka moment. I suddenly realised that the violence was not happening around me, it was happening through me. It was not occurring despite me, it was manifesting because of me.

Excited (and for validation), I checked out the bibles of the world, looked at everything from motivational books about the power of thought, right through to *The Tibetan Book of the Dead* and Dante's *Divine Comedy* and… they all confirmed my suspicion: what I thought about emotively I would create in my life.

Metaphysical self-defence advises us that we attract into our reality what we continually and emotively think about, especially when we experience fear (fear is the perfect example of emotive thinking). It's the law of attraction. So I have learned from concrete experience not to think about, talk about, imagine or ruminate on violence.

Certainly I do not allow myself to fear violence, or I will definitely create it.

I always wanted to be a master thinker, the holy grail of self-control, but my revelation confirmed to me that I was already there. I had always been the man at the helm of my thoughts without even knowing it. I had manifested into my life, through the sheer power of my thoughts, (literally) thousands of people who wanted to fight with me. Thousands. I created nightclubs, pubs, bars, road-rage incidents and arguments in restaurants and at work. I was literally surrounded by violence. I even manifested a huge fight at a friend's christening, because all I thought about was fighting.

On realisation of this I became doubly excited.

I was not aroused by the violence of course, but rather by the power of my thinking.

So, realising that I was a master of manifestation (only, until now I was manifesting all the wrong things), I started to reverse my thinking.

I stopped thinking, talking, watching and partaking in violence, I removed the weapons from every room, emptied my life of any reference, remembrance or residue of violence, and I began thinking about what I did want to attract. I placed powerfully positive books in every room of my house, and started to think emotively about my dream life as a full-time writer. Before long the dream became a trickle that started to birth through the black hole of my imagination. Then the trickle became a steady flow, then the steady flow a gush, and the gush a tsunami of words that shaped themselves into books, plays, articles – at one time I was actually writing for five magazines – and movies.

Before very long the dream was a living reality.

And I had manifested it.

My new-found success did not happen by accident, it happened by design. It was not a stroke of luck, it was a heavily planned campaign. Nobody gifted it to me. I presented it to myself with the power of emotive thinking.

Now, if there is anything in my life that does not fit, I re-tailor it with mentalisation. If my life seems to be going off-track, then I get myself back online in the same way.

Creation is an inside job and you are the one with the schematic. So if you want to change the world, change your thoughts.

Most of all during that time I thought about the one thing that would always beat negativity and violence hands down. Love.

Love

It really does conquer all.

The power of love dissolves all negativity. It is like placing a flashlight on a shadow. Violence cannot live in its presence. Stop seeing enemies. Start seeing fellow human beings: someone's son, someone's brother, someone's husband, someone's daddy. When I was a violent man it was this re-humanisation that brought me to my senses and got me onto a better path. And the re-humanisation occurred because I expanded my intelligence by reading heavily and widely, and also because I started to practise introspection. I would look at some of the limiting beliefs I was holding ('violence is the best way to combat violence', for example) and deeply question them. What I found was that negative traits cannot survive under the light of scrutiny. I questioned everything I was doing. I cross-referenced it with what I had read and with what my intuition was telling me. What I discovered through this mentalisation was that using violence to solve violence did not work (in fact, it actually created more violence). So I stopped being violent and started to look at alternatives. Of all the methods I examined and practised, love brought the best results, but it was also the hardest one to employ because it demanded a higher level of consciousness. Raising our level of consciousness comes through expanding our intellect, deepening our introspection and converting intuitions and ideas into reality with action. Giving love not only dissolves violence, it also creates light for both the giver and the receiver (and also to anyone watching or hearing about your actions). A long time ago, when I was still teaching weekly martial-arts classes and had a large following of students, I remember a potentially violent situation arising that involved another high-profile instructor who had a beef with me. He had been stirring up trouble and spreading negative and untruthful stories about me.

At first I wanted to respond to his verbal violence with physical violence, but after some mentalisation I decided that forgiveness would be a better tool with which to beat this man. I already knew that he would fall easily if I was physically violent with him, because I was a seasoned fighter and he was heavily out of his league (even if he didn't know it). But I also knew that this negative action would not really solve my problem. In fact, in the long run, it would create more problems for me. So I let it go. And when my students – who were sure that I was going to beat this man a new head – asked me what I intended to do, I smiled and told them that I intended to forgive him. To be honest I thought that my students (some of whom were very physical) might think less of me for taking this course of action, but they didn't. They were massively inspired by my example, and promptly started to mimic me, forgiving some of their own enemies. I showed them that violence was the soft option, and that real courage was needed when you entered through the narrow gate. In this instance, the narrow gate was love.

All of this is perhaps new to those with a limited outlook. If it is new to you, then I encourage you to grow. Expand your intelligence by gaining knowledge and converting that knowledge through action. Read challenging books, cross-reference the information with your own experiences and intuition or put the knowledge into action and be the proof. Gaining a holistic knowledge is like expanding your net so you can catch bigger ideas.

An open mind is like bait for light. If you keep your mind closed, you will keep your world dark. Remember it was not long ago that the world was flat and anyone that thought differently courted death.

Create a vacuum. Give as much as you can until you create room for new light. Light quickly dims if you do not give it away (in the form of information, teaching, gifts, love). Light is like the dynamo that needs a turning wheel to keep growing the light.

Chapter 14

Things That Create Light

Getting out of darkness and into light demands a two-pronged assault. If you can consistently practise austerities and meditation – both of which diminish darkness and create light – you will place yourself on the fast track, and success will not only be certain it will also be imminent.

Here are a few of the things that I practise to create light in my life. These enable me to leave dark habit, dark beliefs and ultimately dark realities:

♦ Generosity

♦ Charity

♦ Balance

♦ Service

♦ Love

♦ Silence

♦ Stillness

Generosity

How attractive is generosity! And how rare. There are so few generous people around these days that when you happen upon a genuinely generous soul with no hidden agenda it takes you aback and you find yourself wanting to tell everyone about it. I have a friend who works in a technology company. He was telling me about Bob, their best salesman, and about how he was leagues ahead of everyone else in the company. It seemed he only needed to turn up on the job and people would throw orders and money at him. I was intrigued. I asked my friend: 'So what does Bob do that the rest of you don't?' He didn't know exactly. He said there was no one specific thing he could put his finger on. But as he continued to talk he mentioned how everyone at the office loved Bob, how all his clients loved him and how pretty much everyone that he came into contact with seemed genuinely enamoured of him. I realised then that what it was that Bob had over and above his contemporaries was that he was an extremely generous man. In the canteen he was always treating someone to a meal. In his day-to-day business he was consistently helping the other salesmen with hints and tips and ideas about how they might improve their sales. With his clients he was a beacon of integrity, often delivering more than they were due. Sometimes his generosity even lost him money on an individual sale, but his clients were so delighted with the service that they told all their friends about Bob and many of them brought him their business. Generosity not only brought Bob many friends, it also brought him abundant business.

The opposite is also true.

I bought an expensive piece of jewellery recently. Actually Sharon bought it for me, as a gift to celebrate the completion of our first feature film, *Clubbed*. Now, I have bought a lot of quality jewellery in my time, and I know my way around the salesroom, I know that the price in the shop window always leaves a little room for manoeuvre. So when it came time to complete the purchase, I asked the salesman. How much might he let me have the piece for if I paid cash? He wasn't prepared to budge. Not even a tiny bit. He was arrogantly positive that the piece would sell at the window price, so he would not negotiate. I was quite surprised because, well, there is always a little room. Always. But I didn't push it, and I still bought the jewellery, but I did not go away feeling happy. It was not just because I didn't get a discount (the piece was worth what I paid), it was the fact that I knew the salesman had room to be generous (he had room to give a little) but he chose not to be. It left me feeling like I was shopping in the wrong place. Actually, it left me feeling (rightly or wrongly) that the guy was trying to get as much from me as he could. It certainly didn't leave me feeling enamoured of him. I didn't want to rush out to my friends and say: 'You have got to buy your jewellery from this guy.' Here had been a classic opportunity for a salesman to get a customer for life. As it turned out, he simply got a customer for one sale. And whilst I would never be mean and tell people not to shop with him, I would not go out of my way to recommend him to others.

Even worse is the salesman that is very mean. Not only does he leave one customer dissatisfied, he leaves everyone his customer knows dissatisfied. Because there is one thing you can be sure of: everyone loves to talk about bad service. I have seen directors and writers miss out on lucrative jobs because they were mean to a tea boy on-set ten years ago who now happens to be the head of a big film company, or has become a famous director. I have also been witness to the opposite – people winning amazing opportunities because of a generous (often forgotten) action in their past. I read an article recently in *The Times*. It was in the obituary column, and the man in question was a recently deceased multi-millionaire philanthropist who gave away millions to the homeless and the needy. His generosity was inspired some twenty years before by one single act of kindness. He was young, out of work and out of luck. He could not even raise enough money to eat. One day, out of desperation, he entered a café and ordered a meal that he knew he could not pay for. After he finished the meal, shamefaced, he lied to the waitress and told her he had forgotten his wallet and promised that he would go right to his apartment and bring back the cash (knowing that he could do no such thing). The café owner must have known what was occurring, but he was a compassionate and generous soul. He walked over to the man, handed him $20 said: 'I think you dropped this on the floor sir.' The future philanthropist was overwhelmed, paid for the meal and promised himself that one day he would repay this generosity. Some years later, when he became a millionaire, he went back to the same café, handed the owner $10,000 and said: 'I just wanted to repay you.'

Generosity starts with you, but it has the potential to spread to everyone and bring massively disproportionate returns.

The generous man or woman knows that there is abundance in the world, and they demonstrate that by giving all they can, knowing instinctively that the very act of giving will create a vacuum for a ten-fold return.

And you know what? When you die you lose the lot anyway so you might as well give it away now by choice. Generosity is the world's best-kept secret. Be generous with your time, your energy, your money, your forgiveness, your compassion and your love. It creates light and it brings back more of what you are giving. It creates love. It creates massive abundance. Be an individual and give from the fountain of abundance. If you give generously, you will always have.

Charity

Charity is best served anonymously. The worst statement you will ever hear is: 'I give a lot to charity, but I don't like to talk about it.'

Guess what you just did?

Make your charity anonymous and you will cause the universe to jump with glee. The returns are always better when the investment is secret. Charity (as George Michael so succinctly said) is not a coat you wear twice a year. It is not a box that you can tick to ease your social guilt. It should be done out of love, with no expectation of return or reward or applause. And your generosity will come out eventually anyway. It always does. People will know because – as I've said – true charity is so rare that the recipients will want to tell the whole world. Just don't let the secret slip from your own lips. Charity, again, is not just about coin. In fact, it is more about time (which in each incarnation is finite). Your time is more valuable than money, so when you are charitable with your time, you are really giving. And both generosity and charity create light. Darkness is the ego believing that there is limitation in the universe. Giving to others shrinks the ego and allows the self to shine through.

I was brought up with limitation. I was taught, in all aspects of my life, that there were limitations, and that they should not be challenged. It was not intentional, and it was not mean-spirited. I was simply taught what the folk around me genuinely believed. As an adult I set out to disprove this belief, and I did. Some years ago my belief in abundance was validated after an epiphany. I had a moment of clarity, a union with God. It happened in the middle of the night, shortly after a particularly challenging year when I had stretched myself to new lengths. I won't go into the experience further other than to say that, when it was happening, I knew categorically that something profoundly spiritual was afoot. The details of the epiphany are hard to describe (and so not important in the context of this book) but what is important is what it left me:

the secret to perpetual motion. I actually sat down and I wrote it into a small book called *The Formula* and sent it out to the world as a gift. Not everyone got it, but those who did (those that were ready) really got it. The secret was so simple that I guess some people just could not see it. The secret was service. Giving to others is the secret to perpetual motion. The more you give, the more you get. Every bible tells us so, and every philosophical tablet backs it up.

Prove it and make the knowledge actual by trying it for yourself.

Balance

In the Christian Bible it says that when one stands on a rock he can fight off 1,000 foes, when two stand on a rock together 10,000 foes will flee. This parable is all about unity (or balance) between the conscious and the unconscious, between man and all his parts, and between man and his God.

Balance creates great light. Homeostasis attracts light like a conduit. Lack of balance attracts the greys and the blacks. Balance comes from quiet contemplation and moderation in all things. We might not immediately be aware of what balance is, but we all know when we are out of balance. We have all felt that. What you think, what you say, what you do, what you eat and drink, what you read and watch on the TV or listen to on the radio – all these activities have an effect on your balance because they all affect the adrenals. Excess in any form will trigger the adrenals and place your body into an emergency state.

This state is called the 'sympathetic response' (from the sympathetic nervous system), and is commonly termed the 'fight or flight' syndrome. It is an emergency state that the body takes on in (supposedly) life-threatening situations. The sympathetic nervous system is literally the body out of balance. But it is out of balance for a specific reason. The organism goes on red alert during this time and energy is drawn from all areas of the body (that are seen as non-vital in fight or flight) to aid survival. During arousal your body is dangerously vulnerable because the immune system temporarily closes down and blood pressure rises markedly. Now if this state only occurred infrequently then it would be OK. The adrenals would be raised, we would experience behavioural fight or flight, the danger would be subdued and the body would return to (what is known as) the parasympathetic nervous system – homeostasis. The body is then at balance. The problem is that because people live lives of excess, and excess triggers the adrenals, many people spend much of their lives in a state of high alert with adrenals at full flow and very predatory. Balance is impossible in a predatory state. In a predatory state all we attract is other predators, which is not conducive to light living. It is rather the antithesis of light living. The predatory state is hellish. To be in balance everything has to work in unity together. We all know when we are out of balance, and we should all know that the core of balance starts with right eating. Once correct palate is in place the other senses tend to fall into line and homeostasis becomes the norm. This (to be honest) is a book in itself, so if you get a chance check out my books *Stressbuster* and *Shapeshifter* which go into detail about the sympathetic nervous response and correct palate.

Love

Love is the ultimate in all things light. It is the definitive power.

The problem is that when you make a statement like this it has the tendency to sound wank, as do a lot of philosophical truths when they are translated from definite knowing to inadequate words. Unless you have felt them for yourself, they don't always make complete sense. Often they can sound downright silly. Billy Connolly says that when he is old he intends to stand in church and wait for the priest to say something deeply spiritual like: 'You that are in us and us that are in You… ' And as soon as he does Billy is going to shout: 'Explain!' I get that. It does sound odd. In the book *Siddhartha* (by Herman Hess), a young man (Siddhartha) is searching for enlightenment, but no one that he meets, even the Buddha himself, can articulate quite what enlightenment is, or indeed how one should go about finding it. Siddhartha is sure that someone knows, but for whatever reason they are not prepared to tell him. Later in the book, after a long and arduous journey involving hardship and pain, excess, asceticism and austerities, he eventually finds his own enlightenment. His friend (who Hess calls Siddhartha's 'shadow') Govinda, who has also been on the path his whole life but has been unable to find his way, asks Siddhartha to guide him. He desperately wants to know what his friend has learned, and so he asks him to please impart some wisdom. It is at this point that

Siddhartha realises a great truth: what he has learned does not translate into words. When you try to translate it into words it sounds ridiculous. All he can do is encourage his friend to get back on the path and experience it for himself.

And that is how I know it sounds when you talk about the power of love. It sounds ridiculous. But that does not make it false. It just means it is something that you and me (like Govinda) have to experience for ourselves.

People talk about the power of love so often (in song and in ballad) that it always ends up sounding a little whimsical, a tad trite. Actually it sounds corny. But as a man who has marinated in the top end of the physical, I can stand testament to the fact that the physical is pretty wank and ephemeral compared to the awesome power of love. It is such a difficult emotion to sell as powerful that I am struggling to articulate it. But let me give you an example from my own life.

My son was mugged when he was twelve by a lad of fifteen. The lad took my son's cash (about £10) with menace. When my family came to me with the news, the general consensus was that I should go and find this lad and justifiably bash him up. I am now a spiritually-aware man, but that was not always the case – I do have a heavy background in violence and its gross limitations, and at the time of this mugging I was just starting to see the futility of my violent ways. So I decided to step away from the mob hysteria and the people that wanted claret, preferably served cold, and think this through. In my negative-mind's eye the mugger was a drugged-up, hood-wearing bastard of the first order. That is what I saw, and that is what everyone else around me saw. But I knew that this was an easy stereotype, and I am not a man that likes to take easy solutions. So I reversed my thinking, I delved deeper and tried to find more to this lad than was immediately apparent. A small amount of excavation revealed another picture of the mugger, an all together different image than the one that society had proffered. It was a true picture, the image of what he really was. A boy. He was a boy. He was someone's son, someone's brother, someone's mate. That did not make him suddenly harmless (I know only too well that a fifteen year old with a knife can kill you quicker than cyanide tea), but it did make him human.

This was me using love to solve a situation that would, even a year before, have sent me into a frenzy of violence.

So I found out where the boy lived and I knocked on his door. I decided beforehand that if there was any hostility at all, even the hint of it, I would simply call the police and let the law take over. When the door opened, it was the boy's father. I told him about his son mugging my son, and I told him that I wanted the return of his money along with an apology from the boy. The man was distraught. He told me that his son had gotten into stealing to feed his drug habit, and how it had all but destroyed the lad's mother and had had a catastrophic effect on the whole family. He apologised profusely to me and asked if he could bring the money to my house later that evening. When he arrived later he was with his (very sorry) son and his wife, the boy's mother. She looked wrecked and distraught. Her eyes looked as though they had not seen a dry day for a year. I looked at the lad and in an instant I could foretell his whole future (what little of it there would be), and it did not read well. Even though this lad had mugged my son, all I could feel for him was sadness and love. It was the love that saved the day. It was love that brought the return of my son's money and an end to a sad situation. I could have been physical with him, but that would have led to all sorts of nasty consequences, not least a karmic debt that I would have been forced to repay sometime soon.

Since that day I have tried to see love in everyone I meet, especially in the difficult people. And if I ever have a serious problem with someone, I know that I can change perspective and slay him to pieces with my loving presence.

Love is a force, and in all things mortal it has awesome potential. So practise love for all things and don't get caught up in easy judgement – it is for the sheep, and sheep are not warriors.

Silence and stillness

When I was young and inexperienced (and thought I knew a lot) and people tried to instruct me in meditation as a force of light and power, I used to shake my head and say: 'I don't think so.' I was into Clint Eastwood and Bruce Lee. I was into the physical, which (I thought) was the ultimate problem solver. The very thought of sitting quietly and still was anathema. What was the quiet going to give me but mass boredom? What was stillness going to offer other than frustration? I could not see what the silence and the stillness had to give. I certainly could not see how I might derive power from it. I was like a fly on a TV screen, saying: 'Picture? I don't see a picture.'

When I first started judo I was the same. My instructor Neil Adams – a world renowned judoka – tried to clue me in on the secret to good judo. 'It's all in the grip,' he said. But it meant absolutely nothing to me at all. The grip to me was the hold I took on my opponent's gi (judo suit) so that I could try and throw him. It was just a grip. How could a simple grip be the secret to good Judo? After about eighteen months of full-time training (and after reaching a high standard), I was forced to sit out one session and watch due to an injury. As I observed my training partners in their randori (sparring), that message, the secret, suddenly and inexplicably fell into place and I thought: 'Wow! This game is all in the grip.' The grip was not just the grip. It was the grip! I realised in an instant, that the whole fight was controlled by the person who managed to get a dominant grip on their opponent. A dominant grip meant that you literally controlled the whole fight. If you dominated grip it meant that you were able to execute a throw, almost at will, whilst all your opponent could do was defend. It was amazing how that suddenly dropped in when I least expected it. I have to tell you that it transformed my whole game. Suddenly, players who had once completely dominated me on the mat were now struggling to throw me. And players that I had struggled to throw were going over like old ladies on an icy day. The point is that eighteen months before I had absolutely no idea about the concept of grip, and even when the most respected judoka on this spinning planet tried to give me that information (for free), it meant nothing to me. I couldn't understand him. In short, I had to earn that information myself. I would go as far as to say that the information came to me as a happy accident. What had created that happy accident (that reward) was eighteen months of bollock-breaking mat-work with some of the best talent in the world of judo. The information was worthless until I was able to earn the right to understand the information.

It was exactly the same with quiet and stillness when I first heard about them. They felt weak – even though some of the best yogis and swamis and spiritual behemoths in the world were telling me different. But then, after many years of inner work, I had another happy accident. The concept of power from quiet and stillness hit me like lightning. My happy accident showed me that, to the self, to the Atman (your internal God), quiet and stillness are like nectar. And when you marinate in it consistently, the God in you grows. And as the God in you grows, so the ego (whose nectar is noise, movement, sense stimulation) shrinks. Quiet and stillness are to the Atman what protein is to the bodybuilder, what bricks and mortar are to the construction worker and what love and milk are to the new-born child. When I was able to see it in this light, my whole world changed. I suddenly found purpose in meditation. I could see literal power in stillness (because it brought forward the part that is Ultimate). I could see atonement (or at-one-ment) in mediation.

Silence allows you to expand the self outside the boundary of your corporeal being. It allows you to bathe in light. And once practised, you can find silence even in the noisiest environments. I can find it in a café full of rattling people, I can find it in walks (my wife finds it in window-shopping, but I always think: 'Don't we have enough windows?'). We all find it in different places. My favourite time for it is late at night and at dawn. I love to take a hot drink into the garden and find it there. Once you get into it, it is bliss. And once you become consistent in your practice, you will see your life change in very subtle ways. You will become more open, like an expanding net, and you will catch the most amazing ideas, perceptions and revelations.

When you make the body still so that not even an eyeball moves, you allow light to form all around you. Information is attracted to stillness and all information contains light.

Epilogue

The end already – how quick did that go! Thank you very much for taking the time to invest in yourself with this book. These are some of my findings from a life lived, a life loved and a life that still continues prolifically on and I hope they help you. They have certainly helped me. There is no hypothesis here, just information taken from direct experience and divine sources. It is not intended to enlighten you (that will not happen in a book). It is intended to only crack open the door and allow in a little light. It is intended to open portals into new realities – realities that you can experience. When you experience them this information will be yours to keep. Until you experience it for yourself, they will remain simply words on a page.

Thanks for reading this book. I hope that it catalyses great growth within you. I pray that it will inspire you to deepen your search for light, and help you to escape the dark reality that you may be currently in.

Love, light (and lemonade).

God bless.

Geoff Thompson

www.geoffthompson.com